Drawn by J. Neilson. Eng. by A. B. Durand.

SEAT OF KING PHILIP.

YAMOYDEN

A TALE OF

THE WARS OF KING PHILIP.

Seldon del. Durand sc.

Mount Hope.

NEW YORK,
1820.

YAMOYDEN,

A TALE

OF THE WARS OF KING PHILIP:

IN SIX CANTOS.

BY THE LATE

REV. JAMES WALLIS EASTBURN, A.M.

AND HIS FRIEND.

"All kinds, all creatures stand or fall
By strength of prowess or of wit:
'Tis God's appointment, who shall sway,
And who is to submit.—
Say then that he was wise as brave,
As wise in thought as bold in deed;
For in the principles of things
He sought his moral creed.
And thou, altho' with some wild thoughts,
Wild chieftain of a savage clan!
Had'st this to boast, that thou did'st love
The *liberty* of *man*.".....*Wordsworth.*

NEW-YORK:

PUBLISHED BY JAMES EASTBURN.

Clayton & Kingsland, Printers.

1820.

TO

THE REV.

SAMUEL FARMAR JARVIS, D.D. A.A.S.

RECTOR OF ST. PAUL'S CHURCH, BOSTON,

THIS POEM,

WHICH OWES ITS PUBLICATION, IN A GREAT MEASURE, TO THE FAVOURABLE OPINION EXPRESSED BY HIM OF ITS MERITS,

IS MOST RESPECTFULLY INSCRIBED,

BY

THE EDITOR.

ADVERTISEMENT.

Before submitting this poem to the judgment of the public, it is necessary that the Editor should give a brief account of the manner in which it was composed. He hopes that this will prove, to the candid and intelligent, a sufficient apology for the defects with which, he is well aware, this juvenile production abounds.

It was written, in separate portions, by the late Rev. James Wallis Eastburn, and himself, during the winter of 1817—18, and the following spring. Mr. Eastburn, in 1816, went to Bristol, Rhode-Island, to pursue the study of divinity, under the direction of the Rt. Rev. A. V. Griswold, Bishop of the Eastern Diocess. He was constantly in the habit of amusing his hours of relaxation, with poetical composition; and the local traditions connected with the scenery, in his immediate vicinity, suggested to him a fit subject for his favourite employment. He often mentioned, in the course of his correspondence with the Editor, his intention of making some of the adventures of King Philip, the well known Sachem of Pokanoket, the theme of a poetical romance. In the year following when he visited New-York, the plan of the proposed story was drawn up, in conjunction. We had then read nothing on the subject; and our plot was formed from a hasty glance into a few pages of Hubbard's Narrative. To quote a simile from that crude historian, we began, like bad heralds, to meddle with the charge, before we had blazoned the field; and, though the action of our fable only occupied the space of forty-eight hours, we were led into several inconsistencies, in the general outline first proposed; from which no departure was afterwards made. After Mr. Eastburn's return to Bristol, the poem was written, according to the parts severally assigned; and transmitted, reciprocally, in the course of correspondence. It was commenced in November, 1817, and finished before the summer of 1818; except the concluding Stanzas of the Sixth Canto, which were added after Mr. Eastburn left Bristol. As the fable was defective, from our ignorance of the subject, the execution was also, from the same cause, and the hasty mode of composition, in every respect imperfect. Mr. Eastburn was then preparing to take orders; and his studies, with that view, engrossed his attention. He was ordained in October, 1818. Between that time and the period of his going to Accomack county, in Virginia, whence he had received an invitation to take charge of a congregation, he transcribed the two first Cantos of this Poem, with but few material variations, from the first collating copy. The labours of his ministry left him no time, even for his most delightful amusement. He had made no further progress in the correction of the work, when he returned to this city, in July, 1819. His health was then so much impaired, that writing of any kind was too great a labour. He had packed up the manuscripts, intending to finish his second copy in Santa Cruz, whither it was recommended to him to go, as the last resource, to recruit his exhausted constitution. He died on the fourth day of his passage, December 2d, 1819.

He left among his papers a great quantity of poetry, of which his part of "Yamoyden" forms but a small proportion. His friends may think proper, at some future period, to make selections from his miscellaneous remains, and arrange them for publication. It was their wish, however, that this poem might be first published, and they were determined in that wish, by the approbation of a gentleman whose talents and learning are universally respected in this community. The Editor was therefore induced to comply with their request, and undertake the correction of the manuscript. His labour, in so doing, has not been trifling. He had no right to make any alterations in the original plot; or to destroy his deceased friend's poetical identity. He has endeavoured to remove as many errors, in point of matter or expression, as was consistent with these necessary restraints. From looking over several books, whose subjects were connected with that of the poem, he has been led to make some additions to the original matter. The principal of these, in point of bulk, are,—the verses in the commencement, relating to the previous history of the Indian wars;—the Sermon introduced in the third Canto;—the Ode to the Manitto of Dreams, in the fourth;—and the introduction of the Mohegan, in the fifth and sixth. The last alteration was always contemplated by Mr. Eastburn, who had made the heroine perform the journey alone. The Editor mentions these portions as his own, because they were hastily added in the course of transcription, and printed as soon as written; and if they are defective, the discredit should attach to himself alone. The particular property in the rest of the poem, belonging to each author, it would be endless to particularize. Notice is taken in the notes of many errors, the principal of which is the subject of the fourth Canto. The few notes marked E. were found among Mr. Eastburn's papers. The rest have been added by the Editor.

> Plura, quidem, mandare tibi, si quæris habebam;
> Sed vereor tardæ causa fuisse moræ.
> Quod si, quæ subeunt, tecum, liber, omnia ferres,
> Sarcina laturo magna futurus eras.

The Poem, in the main, is still to be considered as having been written three years ago; when the age of Mr. Eastburn was twenty, and that of the Editor eighteen years. The latter had scarce attempted versification, of any kind, from the time when the draught of "Yamoyden" was finished: and nothing but the circumstances he has stated, could have induced him to resume the practice, or appear as the author of a poem. As to his individual reputation, on that score, he believes, he is sincerely and perfectly indifferent: but it would be folly to deny, that he could not, without pain, see this joint production, now consecrated in his memory by the death of his friend, meet with unfair criticism or sullen neglect.

He cannot conclude without returning his sincere acknowledgments to those gentlemen, who have taken an interest in the publication; by whose kindness he has been enabled to consult such books as he was in need of. He can only hope that their favourable expectations may not be disappointed.

November 20th, 1820.

PROEM.

GO FORTH, sad fragments of a broken strain,
The last that either bard shall e'er essay!
The hand can ne'er attempt the chords again,
That first awoke them, in a happier day:
Where sweeps the ocean breeze its desert way,
His requiem murmurs o'er the moaning wave;
And he who feebly now prolongs the lay,
Shall ne'er the minstrel's hallowed honours crave;
His harp lies buried deep, in that untimely grave!

Friend of my youth! with thee began the love
Of sacred song; the wont, in golden dreams,
Mid classic realms of splendours past to rove,
O'er haunted steep, and by immortal streams;
Where the blue wave, with sparkling bosom gleams
Round shores, the mind's eternal heritage,
For ever lit by memory's twilight beams;
Where the proud dead, that live in storied page,
Beckon, with awful port, to glory's earlier age.

There would we linger oft, entranc'd, to hear,
O'er battle fields, the epic thunders roll;
Or list, where tragic wail upon the ear,
Through Argive palaces shrill echoing, stole;
There would we mark, uncurbed by all control,
In central heaven, the Theban eagle's flight;
Or hold communion with the musing soul
Of sage or bard, who sought, mid Pagan night,
In lov'd Athenian groves, for truth's eternal light.

Homeward we turned, to that fair land, but late
Redeemed from the strong spell that bound it fast,
Where Mystery, brooding o'er the waters, sate
And kept the key, till three millenniums past;
When, as creation's noblest work was last,
Latest, to man it was vouchsafed, to see
Nature's great wonder, long by clouds o'ercast,
And veiled in sacred awe, that it might be
An empire and a home, most worthy for the Free.

And here, forerunners strange and meet were found,
Of that blest freedom, only dreamed before;—
Dark were the morning mists, that lingered round
Their birth and story, as the hue they bore.
"Earth was their Mother;"—or they knew no more,
Or would not that their secret should be told;
For they were grave and silent; and such lore,
To stranger ears, they loved not to unfold,
The long-transmitted tales, their sires were taught of old.

Kind nature's commoners, from her they drew
Their needful wants, and learnt not how to hoard;
And him whom strength and wisdom crowned, they knew,
But with no servile reverence, as their lord.
And on their mountain summits they adored
One great, good Spirit, in his high abode,
And thence their incense and orisons poured
To his pervading presence, that abroad
They felt through all his works,—their Father, King, and God.

And in the mountain mist, the torrent's spray,
The quivering forest, or the glassy flood,
Soft falling showers, or hues of orient day,
They imaged Spirits beautiful and good;
But when the tempest roared, with voices rude,
Or fierce, red lightning fired the forest pine,
Or withering heats untimely seared the wood,
The angry forms they saw of powers malign;
These they besought to spare, those blest for aid divine.

As the fresh sense of life, through every vein,
With the pure air they drank, inspiring came,
Comely they grew, patient of toil and pain,
And, as the fleet deer's, agile was their frame;
Of meaner vices scarce they knew the name;
These simple truths went down from sire to son,—
To reverence age,—the sluggish hunter's shame,
And craven warrior's infamy, to shun,—
And still avenge each wrong, to friends or kindred done.

From forest shades they peered, with awful dread,
When, uttering flame and thunder from its side,
The ocean-monster, with broad wings outspread,
Came, ploughing gallantly the virgin tide.
Few years have past, and all their forests' pride
From shores and hills has vanished, with the race,
Their tenants erst, from memory who have died,
Like airy shapes, which eld was wont to trace,
In each green thicket's depths, and lone, sequestered place.

And many a gloomy tale Tradition yet
Saves from oblivion, of their struggles vain,
Their prowess and their wrongs, for rhymer meet,
To people scenes, where still their names remain;
—And so began our young, delighted strain,
That would evoke the plumed chieftains brave,
And bid their martial hosts arise again,
Where Narragansett's tides roll by their grave,
And Haup's romantic steeps are piled above the wave.

Friend of my youth! with thee began my song,
And o'er thy bier its latest accents die;
Misled in phantom-peopled realms too long,—
Though not to me the muse averse deny,
Sometimes, perhaps, her visions to descry,—
Such thriftless pastime should with youth be o'er;
And he who loved with thee his notes to try,
But for thy sake, such idlesse would deplore,—
And swears to meditate the thankless muse no more.

But, no! the freshness of that past shall still
Sacred to memory's holiest musings be;
When through the ideal fields of song, at will,
He roved, and gathered chaplets wild with thee;
When, reckless of the world, alone and free,
Like two proud barks, we kept our careless way,
That sail by moonlight o'er the tranquil sea;
Their white apparel and their streamers gay,
Bright gleaming o'er the main, beneath the ghostly ray;—

And downward, far, reflected in the clear,
Blue depths, the eye their fairy tackling sees;
So, buoyant, they do seem to float in air,
And silently obey the noiseless breeze;—
Till, all too soon, as the rude winds may please,
They part, for distant ports: Thee gales benign
Swift wafting, bore, by Heaven's all-wise decrees,
To its own harbour sure, where each divine
And joyous vision, seen before in dreams, is thine.

Muses of Helicon! melodious race
Of Jove and golden-haired Mnemosyné!
Whose art from memory blots each sadder trace,
And drives each scowling form of grief away!
Who, round the violet fount, your measures gay
Once trod, and round the altar of great Jove;
Whence, wrapt in silvery clouds, your nightly way
Ye held, and ravishing strains of music wove,
That soothed the Thunderer's soul, and filled his courts above!

Bright choir! with lips untempted, and with zone
Sparkling, and unapproached by touch profane;
Ye, to whose gladsome bosoms ne'er was known
The blight of sorrow, or the throb of pain;—
Rightly invoked,—if right the elected swain,
On your own mountain's side ye taught of yore,
Whose honoured hand took not your gift in vain,
Worthy the budding laurel-bough it bore,—*
Farewell! a long Farewell! I worship you no more!

* *Hesiod. Theog.* l. 1. 60. 30.

YAMOYDEN.

INTRODUCTION.

Stat vetus et multos incœdua sylva per annos;
Credibile est illi numen inesse loco.

Hark to that shriek upon the summer blast!
Wildly it swells the fitful gusts between,
And as its dying echoes faint have past,
Sad moans the night-wind o'er the troubled scene.
Sunk is the day, obscured the valleys green;
Nor moon, nor stars are glimmering in the sky,
Thick veiled behind their tempest-gathered screen;
Lost in deep shades the hills and waters lie;
Whence rose that boding scream, that agonizing cry?

Spirit of Eld! who, on thy moss-clad throne,
Record'st the actions of the mighty dead;
By whom the secrets of the past are known,
And all oblivion's spell-bound volume read;—
Sleep wo and crime beneath thine awful tread?

Or is it but idle fancy's mockery vain,
Who loves the mists of wonder round to spread?
No! 'tis a sound of sadder, sterner strain,
Spirit of by-gone years, that haunts thine ancient
reign!

'Tis the death wail of a departed race,—
Long vanished hence, unhonoured in their grave;
Their story lost to memory, like the trace
That to the greensward erst their sandals gave;
—Wail for the feather-cinctured warriors brave,
Who, battling for their fathers' empire well,
Perished, when valour could no longer save
From souless bigotry, and avarice fell,
That tracked them to the death, with mad, infuriate
yell.

Spirit of Eld! inspire one generous verse,
The unpractised minstrel's tributary song;
Mid these thine ancient groves he would rehearse
The closing story of their Sachem's wrong.

On that rude column, shrined thy wrecks among,
Tradition! names there are, which time hath worn,
Nor yet effaced; proud names, to which belong
A dismal tale of foul oppressions borne,
Which man can ne'er recall, but which the muse
    may mourn.

YAMOYDEN.

CANTO FIRST.

I.

The morning air was freshly breathing,
The morning mists were wildly wreathing;
Day's earliest beams were kindling o'er
The wood-crowned hills and murmuring shore.
'Twas summer; and the forests threw
Their chequered shapes of varying hue,
In mingling, changeful shadows seen,
O'er hill and bank, and headland green.
Blithe birds were carolling on high
Their matin music to the sky,
As glanced their brilliant hues along,
Filling the groves with life and song;
All innocent and wild and free
Their sweet, ethereal minstrelsy.

The dew drop sparkled on the spray,
Danced on the wave the inconstant ray;
And moody grief, with dark control,
There only swayed the human soul!

II.

With equal swell, above the flood,
The forest-cinctured mountain stood;
Its eastward cliffs, a rampart wild,
Rock above rock sublimely piled.
What scenes of beauty met his eye,
The watchful sentinel on high!
With all its isles and inlets lay
Beneath, the calm, majestic bay;
Like molten gold, all glittering spread,
Where the clear sun his influence shed;
In wreathy, crispëd brilliance borne,
While laughed the radiance of the morn.
Round rocks, that from the headlands far
Their barriers reared, with murmuring war,
The chafing stream, in eddying play,
Fretted and dashed its foamy spray;

Along the shelving sands its swell
With hushed and equal cadence fell;
And here, beneath the whispering grove,
Ran rippling in the shadowy cove.
Thy thickets with their liveliest hue,
Aquetnet green! were fair to view;
Far curved the winding shore, where rose
Pocasset's hills in calm repose;
Or where descending rivers gave
Their tribute to the ampler wave.
Emerging frequent from the tide,
Scarce noticed mid its waters wide,
Lay flushed with morning's roseate smile,
The gay bank of some little isle;
Where the lone heron plumed his wing,
Or spread it as in act to spring,
Yet paused, as if delight it gave
To bend above the glorious wave.

III.

Where northward spread the unbounded scene,
Oft, in the valley's bosom green,

The hamlets' mouldering ruins showed,
Where war with dæmon brand had strode.
By prostrate hedge and fence o'erthrown,
And fields by blackening hillocks known,
And leafless tree, and scattered stone,
The midnight murderer's work was shown,
Oft melting in the distant view
The cot sent up its incense blue,
As yet unwrapt by hostile fire;
And, mid its trees, some rustic spire,
A peaceful signal, told that there
Was sought the God of peace in prayer.
The Wampanoag from the height
Of Haup, who strained his anxious sight,
To mark if foes their covert trace,
Beheld, and curst the Christian race!

IV.

Now two score years of peace had past,
Since in the west the battle yell
Was borne on every echoing blast,
Until the Pequots' empire fell;

And SASSACOUS, now no more,
Lord of a thousand bowmen, fled;
And all the chiefs, his boast before,
Were mingled with the unhonoured dead.
Sannap and Sagamore were slain,
On Mystic's banks, in one red night;
The once far-dreaded king in vain
Sought safety in inglorious flight;
And reft of all his regal pride,
By the fierce Maqua's hand he died.
Long o'er the land, with cloudless hue,
Had peace outspread her skies of blue;
The blood-stained axe was buried long;
Till METACOM his war-dance held,
And round the flaming pyre the song
Of vengeance and of death was yelled.
The steeps of Haup reverbed afar
The Wampanoägs' shout for war;
Fiercely they trim their crested hair,
The sanguine battle stains prepare,
And martial gear, while over all
Proud waves the feathery coronal.

Their peäg belts are girt for fight,
Their loaded pouches slung aright,
The musket's tube is bright and true,
The tomahawk's edge is sharped anew,
And counsels stern, and flashing eyes
Betoken dangerous enterprise.

V.

The red fire is blazing; ring compassing ring,
They whirled in the war-dance, and circuiting sing;
And the chieftains, in turn to the pile as they go,
In each brand saw a warrior, each gleed was a foe;
Revenge on the whites and their allies they swear,
Mohegans, Niantics and Pequots they dare,
And slay in the dream of their ire;
The hills of Pocasset replied to the call,
And their QUEEN sent her chiefs and her warriors all,
To the rites of the lurid fire.

VI.

Thro' Narraganset's countless clan
The secret wildfire circling ran;

In northern wilds, the gathering word
The tributary Nipnets heard.
Busy and quick, to their errand true,
The messengers of mischief flew,
Noiseless as speeds the painted dart,
In the thicket's shade, to the quarry's heart,
That scares not in its passage fleet
The woodland hosts from their green retreat.

VII.

But SAUSAMAN untimely slain,
Kindled too soon the fatal train.
From where with mild, majestic pride,
Their peaceful, and abounding tide
Quunihticut's broad waters pour
Even to the ocean's sounding shore—
Began one universal strife,
One murderous hunt for human life.
The wexing moon oft waned anew,
Ere grass upon the war-path grew:
On every gale the war-whoop rung;
From every grove the ambush sprung;

The hamlet's blaze, the midnight yell,
Ceased not the desperate strife to tell,
Till o'er the land, with blood defiled,
Went forth a voice of wailing wild;
A voice of mourning and of pain,
Their youngest and their bravest slain.

VIII.

Full high the savage pride was raised,
Till Narraganset's fortress blazed.
When bleak December sheeted o'er
The wilderness with mantle hoar,
Reckless within their hold assailed,
They saw the avenging army pour,
Beheld their boasted bulwarks scaled.
The whitemen made their entrance good,
All slippery with their comrades' blood;
A thousand wigwams kindled sent
Their glare along the firmament;
The sun declining from his noon,
Faded, a dim, wan circle soon;

The heavens, around that lurid light,
Frowned like the realms of central night;
Far, far around, the gleening snow
Was ruddy with the unnatural glow;
Where the dun column wreathing rolled,
Red flowed the river's tides below.
Amid the slaughtered, in their hold,
Stifling, in vain their warriors bold
Each blazing sconce in fury sought,
Poured on the foe their deadly shot,
Or in mad leaps of torture broke
Thro' sulphurous fire and volumed smoke;—
While uproar, flame and deafening yell
Made the scene seem the vault of hell,
Where, writhing wild in penance dire,
Fiends danced mid pyramids of fire!
Nor ceased the musket roar, the shout,
The obstreperous clamours of the rout,
Till gathering night with shades profound
Of gloom and horror closed around.
Tracked by their blood along the snow,
Returned the victors, sad and slow;—
But, where the smoking ruins show

The prostrate citadel—one heap
Of smouldering ashes, broad and deep,
Where friend or husband none may trace,
The pride of Narraganset's race,
The grisly trophy of the fray,
A holocaust for freedom lay!

IX.

Stabbed in the heart of all their power,
The voice of triumph from that hour
Rose faintly, mid the heathen host,
Sunk was their pride, and quelled their boast.
Broken and scattering wide and far,
Feebly they yet maintained the war.
Spring came; on blood alone intent,
Men o'er her flowers regardless went;
Thro' cedar grove and thicket green,
The serried steel was glistening sheen;
Earth lay untilled; the deadly chase
Ceased not of that devoted race,
Till of the tribes whose rage at first
In one o'erwhelming deluge burst,

No trace the inquiring eye could find,
Save in the ruins left behind.
Like wintry torrent they had poured,
O'er mounds and rocks it raved and roared,
Dashed in blind fury where it broke
In showery spray and wavy smoke;
And now, sad vestige of its wrath,
Alone was left its wasted path.

X.

Stark thro' the dismal fens they lie,
Or on the felon gibbet high
Their mangled members hung proclaim
Their constancy—their conquerors' shame.
Ah! happier they, who in the strife
For freedom fell, than o'er the main,
Those who in slavery's galling chain
Still bore the load of hated life,—
Bowed to base tasks their generous pride,
And scourged and broken-hearted died!
The remnant of the conquered band,
Submissive, at the victors' hand,

As for a boon of mercy, crave
A shred of all their Fathers' land,
A transient shelter and a grave.
Or far where boundless lakes expand,
With weary feet the exiles roam,
Until their tawny brethren gave
The persecuted race a home.

XI.

But METACOM, the cause of all,
Last of his host, was doomed to fall.
Unconquered yet, when at his side
His boldest and his wisest died;
When all whom kin or friendship made
To his fallen fortunes dear were dead;
Beggared in wealth and power; pursued
A sentenced wretch, thro' swamp and wood;—
Yet he escaped—tho' he might hear
The hunters' uproar round him wake,
And bullets whispered death was near:
O'er bank and stream, thro' grove and brake
He led them, fleet as mountain deer,

Nor yet his limbs had learned to quake,
Nor his heart caught the taint of fear.

XII.

His covert to his foes unknown,
With such worn train as war had spared,
Once more to Haup the chief repaired,
Of all his line the home and throne.
There, where the spirits of the dead
Seemed flitting through each moonlight glade,—
Where pageant hosts of glory fled
In mockery rose with vain parade,—
In gloomy grandeur o'er his head,
Where forests cast congenial shade,—
Brooding mid scenes of perished state,
He mused to madness on his fate.
South from the tarlëd swamp that spread
Below the mount, an upland rose;
Where towering elms all gray with eld,
And birchen thickets close concealed
The hunted race from quest of foes.

Beneath, their screen the elders threw,
And fern and bramble rankly grew;
By simple nature wisely taught
Such covert still the savage sought:
So in her leafy form the hare
Sits couched and still, when down the gale,
Of hounds and horns the mingling blare
She hears in tones of terror swell.
So spreads, beneath the liquid surge,
To shun the approaching monster's gorge,
The wary fish its inky blood,
And dies with rayless hue the flood.

XIII.

Beside the mountain's rugged steeps,
The SACHEM now his council keeps;
Though straightened in that hopeless stound,
Begirt with fear and famine round,
Resolved himself on daring deed,
He listened reckless of their rede.
Once more within their ancient hold,
How dwindled from their pomp of old!

Toilworn and few and doubtful met
The PANIESE in their council state.
High rose the cliffs; but proud above
The regal oaks their branches fling,
Arching aloft with verdant cove,
Where thick their leaves they interwove,
Fit canopy for woodland king.
Vines, with tenacious fibres, high
Clomb o'er those rocks luxuriantly;
Oft o'er their rugged masses gray,
With rustling breeze the wild flowers play;
While at the base their purple hues,
Impearled with morning's glittering dews,
Bloomed round the pile of rifted stone,
Which, as in semblance of a throne,
The hand of Nature there had placed;
And rambling wild, where lower still
Bubbled and welled a sparkling rill,
These simple flowers its margin graced.
Clear as the brightest steel to view,
Thro' mossy turf of greenest hue,

Its lymph that gushing fountain spread :—
And still through ages since have sped,
  That little spring is seen ;
It bears his name whose deeds of dread
  Disturbed its margin green ;
As pure, as full, its waters rise,
While those who once its peace profaned,
Have past, and to the stranger's eyes
Nor trace nor memory hath remained.
Smooth lay the turf before the seat,
Sprinkled with flow'rets fair and sweet ;
The violet and the daisy gay,
And goldcups bright like spangles lay.
Thick round the glade the forest grew,
Whose quivering leaves and pillars through,
The eye might catch the sparkling ray,
Where sea-gulls wheeled in mazy play.

XIV.

There met the council, round the throne,
Where he, in power, in thought alone,

Not like the sentenced outlaw sate,
The abandoned child of wayward fate,
But as of those tall cliffs a part,
Cut by some bolder sculptor's art,—
The imaged God, erect and proud,
To whom the simple savage bowed.
His was the strength the weak that sways;
The glance the servile herd obeys;
The brow of majesty, where thought
And care their deepest lines had wrought,
And told, like furrows broad that mark
The giant ash-tree's fretted bark,
How stormy years, with forceful sway,
Will wear youth's scarless gloss away.
Shorn were his locks, whose ample flow
Had else revealed him to the foe;
And travel-stained the beaver spoils,
That sheathed his martial limbs below.
But seemed it that he yet would show,
Even mid the hunter's closing toils,
Some splendours of his former state,
When in his royalties he sate.

For round his brow, with symbols meet,
In wampum wrought with various die,
Entwined a studded coronet,
With circling plumage waving high.
Above his stalworth shoulders set
A feathery-woven mantle lay,
Where many-tinctured pinions gay
Sprinkled the raven's plumes of jet.
Collar beneath and gorget shone,
The peäg armlets and the zone,
That round with fretted shell-work graced,
Clipped with broad ring his shapely waist.
And all war's dread caparison,
Horn, pouch and tomahawk were slung;
And wide and far descending hung,
Quaintly embossed with bird and flower,
The belt that marked the SACHEM's power.

XV.

Know ye the Indian warrior race?
How their light form springs in strength and grace,

Like the pine on their native mountain side,
That will not bow in its deathless pride;
Whose rugged limbs of stubborn tone
No flexuous power of art will own,
But bend to Heaven's red bolt alone!
How their hue is deep as the western die
That fades in Autumn's evening sky;
That lives for ever upon their brow,
In the summer's heat, and the winter's snow;
How their raven locks of tameless strain,
Stream like the desert courser's mane:
How their glance is far as the eagle's flight,
And fierce and true as the panther's sight:
How their souls are like the crystal wave,
Where the spirit dwells in his northern cave;
Unruffled in its caverned bed,
Calm lies its glimmering surface spread;
Its springs, its outlet unconfest,
The pebble's weight upon its breast
Shall wake its echoing thunders deep,
And when their muttering accents sleep,

Its dark recesses hear them yet,
And tell of deathless love or hate!

XVI.

The council met; each bosom there
Pregnant with doubt or with despair;
And each wan eye and hollow cheek
The waste of toil and famine speak;
Yet o'er the dew-webbed turf reclined,
Silent they sate; and stranger's eye
Had deemed, in idle mood resigned
To nature's sweet tranquillity,
They lay to catch the mingling sound
Of woods and waters murmuring round;—
That the robin carolling blithe they heard,
Or the breeze the shivering leaves that stirred.
Among their eagle plumes it played,
And with their cinctures dalliance made;
But customed were they to control
The cradled whirlwinds of the soul;
And calm was every warrior's mien,
As if there a feast of love had been.

XVII.

Ill could the fiery Sachem brook
That gloomy, never-changing look.
Tho' long inured to mazy wile,
Through all the thousand lakes of guile,
His secret skiff had held its course
And shunned each torrent's eddying force,
Yet ever would the fiery soul
  Through all the circles dart,
Which, like the ice around the pole,
  Begirt the Indian heart.

XVIII.

Up started Metacom ;—the train
Of all his wrongs,—his perished power,—
His blasted hopes,—his kindred slain,—
His quenchless hate which blazed in vain,
So fierce in its triumphant hour,
But now to his own heart again
Withdrawn, but ran like liquid flame
Boiling through all his fevered frame,—
All, all seemed rushing on his brain :—

Each trembling fibre told the strife,
Which quelled that storm with madness rife,
Gathering in horrors o'er his brow,
And flashing wildly bright below.
While o'er his followers faint and few,
On inquest stern his glances flew,
Across his quivering lips in haste
A smile of bitterness there past;—
As if a beam from the lamp had stole
That burnt within his inmost soul,
As in a deep, sepulchral cell,—
It seemed with transient curl to tell,
How in his triumph or his fall,
He doubted and he scorned them all!
But silence straight the SACHEM broke,
And thus his taunt abrupt he spoke—

XIX.

"Still do we live? to yonder skies
Yet does our warm breath buoyant rise,—
To that Great Spirit, who ne'er inhales
Incense from all the odorous gales,

In the world of warrior souls, more blest,
Than that respired from the freeman's breast!
Yet do we live? or struck by fear,
As the wretch by subtle sorcerer near,
Palsied and pining, must we lie
In yon dark fen, and dimly spy
Our fathers' hills, our native sky:—
Like the coward ghosts, whom the bark of stone
Leaves in the eternal wave to moan,
And wail for ever, as they descry
The blissful isle they can come not nigh;
Where the souls of the brave from toil released,
Prolong the chase, the dance, the feast,
And fill the sparkling chalice high,
From the springs of immortality!
Say, has oblivion kindly come,
To veil remembrance in its gloom?
Have ye forgot, that whilome here,
Your fathers drove the bounding deer;
When now, so works the Evil One,
Like heartless deer their children run;—
Or trembling in their darksome lair,

While fear's cold dews gush full and fast,
One venturous glance no longer dare
Round on their native forests cast.
The hunters came, the charm they brought;
The tempting lure the senseless sought,
And tamely to the spoiler gave
The ancient birthright of the brave!

XX.

"Oblivion? O! the films of age
Shall shroud yon sun's resplendent eye,
And waning in his pilgrimage,
His latest beam in heaven shall die,
Ere on the soil from whence we fled,
The story of our wrongs be dead!
Could the tall trunk of peace once more
Lift its broad foliage on our shore;
And on the beaver robe outspread
Our remnant rest beneath its shade;
From stainless bowls send incense high
Amid the blue and cloudless sky;

Mark round us waves unrimpled flow,
And o'er green paths no bramble grow;—
Say where in earth profoundly deep,
Should all our wrongs in darkness sleep?
What art the sod shall o'er them heap;
And rear the tree whose verdant tower
Aloft shall build, beneath embower,—
Till men shall pass and shall not know
The secrets foul that rest below?
The memory ne'er can die, of all
For blood, for vengeance that can call,
While feels a red man in his breast
The might, the soul his sires possest,
Toil, death and danger can defy,
Look up to heaven, and proudly cry,
Eternal and Almighty One,
Father of all! I am thy son!

XXI.

"Poor, crouching children of the brave!
Lo! where the broad and sparkling wave

Anointed once the freeman's shore,
Your fathers' tents arise no more.
There lie your masters in their pride;
And not so thick, o'er torpid tide,
The blessed light that beams on earth
Warms the coiled vipers into birth,
And not so loathsome do they spread
Their slime along its sedgy bed,
As glittering on my aching eyes,
The white man's homes accursëd rise!
I rave;—and ye are cold and tame;
Forget ye MASSASOIET's shame?
Forget ye him, who, snared and caught,
Soared on the chainless wings of thought,
A lowly captive might not be,
For his heart broke, and he was free!
Last, poorest of a mighty race,
Proscribed, devoted to the chase,
I hold this cumbrous load of life,
  Avenging powers! from you;
The remnant of its dreary strife
  To hoarded vengeance due!

But ye—live on; and lowly kneel,
And crouching kiss the impending steel,
Which, in mere weariness of toil,
Full sated with your kinsmen's spoil,
May haply grant the boon to live;—
For this your cringing *taubut* give;
And o'er your father's hallowed grave
Drag the foul members of the slave!
O slaves! the children of the free!
The hunted brute cries shame on ye!
At bay each threatening horn he turns,
As fierce the enclosing circle burns;—
And ye are baited in your lair,
And will ye fight not for despair?"

XXII.

Thus spoke the Sachem in his ire,
Bright anger blazing in his eye;
And, as the bolt of living fire
Streams through the horrors of the sky,
Kindling the pine, whose flames aspire
In one red pyramid on high,

In all his warriors, as he spoke,
The rising fury fiercely woke;
Each tomahawk, in madness swayed,
Gleamed mid the forest's quivering shade;
Loud rose the war-whoop, wild and shrill;
The frowning rock, the towering hill
  Prolonged the indignant cry:
Far o'er the stilly æther borne,
By the light pinions of the morn,
It fell on the lonely traveller's ear,
Round on the wilderness in fear
  He gazed with anxious eye;
On distant wave the wanderer well
Knew the loud larum terrible,
And trembled at the closing swell,
  As slow its echoes die.

XXIII.

" 'Tis well—no more," the SACHEM said,
" The Spirit hears your answer made.
But who art thou, whose arm alone
  Hangs nerveless at thy side?

Who mak'st thyself mid warriors one,
And, dog-like, hast no single tone,
  To swell their shout of pride?
Son of a base and recreant band!
Who from the common tyrant's hand,
Took the war-hatchet, blood-died pledge
Of peace between them and our foe,
And proved too well how keen its edge;—
Its temper well their brethren know.
MIANTONIMO'S honoured head
Our laggard vengeance will upbraid;—
CANONCHET and PANOQUIN, slain
By coward hands, look forth in vain,
From their eternal towers, to spy
Mohegan ghosts go wandering by;—
For blood a thousand heroes cry,
Whose bones, untombed, dishonoured lie:
No kindred hands, with reverent care,
Those relics from the waste shall bear;
Ne'er from his path shall traveller turn,
Beside their grassy mound to mourn;

Nor, prostrate stretched beside their grave,
Sighing shall say—there sleep the brave!
And shalt thou live, and mingle here
With those their memory who revere?"

XXIV.

Young Agamoun, by many a snare
Of fame, revenge and promise fair,
Long since from the Mohegan shore
The Sachem and his warriors bore:
Then the young hero's heart beat high,
With all the patriot's sympathy;—
Fierce as the battle god, for fight
Collecting his unconquered might,
Along the war-path of the heaven,
Revealed in red and sulphurous levin,
Rolling his gloomy clouds afar,
Exulting at the scent of war;—
So he went forth, in strength and youth,
And hailed hope's paltering form as truth:
But years had passed since hope grew cold;
False was the fraudful tale she told;

Ambition's dream and promise high
Were but the song of birds flown by!
He saw his marshalled tribe oppose
Their brethren, as their mortal foes;
He saw their scanted numbers fail,
Like autumn's leaves on winter's gale;
Until, his hopes, his followers gone,
The western chief remained alone.
Mistrust and jealousy had torn
A noble heart by fortune worn;
From council and from power estranged,
He saw the SACHEM's visage changed;
The silver chain, in earthly dust,
Had caught the stains of human rust;
Till in the hour of adverse fate,
Its links were snapt for e'er by hate.

XXV.

So where at first, with gurgling rush,
The founts of mighty rivers gush,
So near the kindred streamlets flow,
Their pebbly channels murmuring through,

Their distance at a stride the child
May measure, as he gambols wild:
Each, mingling with its countless tides,
O'er earth's unequal bosom glides,
Through adverse climes and distant realms,—
And when their tribute ocean whelms,
With stranger name each stream appears,
Disgorged in different hemispheres.
Untainted yet, by crime and wo,
While nature's generous currents flow,
Thro' sympathy's luxuriant mould,
Hearts, side by side, their course may hold;
But parted on the wastes of time,
How soon forgot that earlier clime!

XXVI.

"Speak! traitor, speak! thy thoughts unfold!
Be thy cloaked treasons instant told!
Whizzes in air the venomed dart,
Ere yet it rankles in the heart;—
Prepared to sting the lurking snake
His monitory hiss will wake;—
Hiss, serpent, hiss!"

The Sachem spoke:
Resentment rising seemed to choke
The words of wrath that forth had broke:
But conscience lent her bland relief,
And calmly spoke the injured chief.
—"Whate'er of private feud my heart
To my tongue's language might impart,
I learnt to bury and to hide,
When battling on my country's side.
Who, when her sacred cause inspires,
Enkindles at polluted fires,
Where unclean spirits hold retreat,
Where none but the impure may meet,
His passions base, revenge or pride,—
Curst be that guilty parricide!
O noteless in the songs of fame,
A beacon blaze his recreant name!
Hovering for ever may it be
O'er the dull fens of infamy!
The stem must crack—the cause must fail,
If such unholy warmth prevail!

But wherefore more? ye've known me long,
Ye saw me when your cause was strong—
Ye proved me when your hopes were weak,
If ye have found me wanting, speak!

XXVII.

"Here if we linger, what remains?
Inglorious death, accursëd chains!
Ah! tho' the bleak and sheeted blast
Round Haup's bare cliffs its shroud shall cast,
And sweep in howling, wild affray
The sere and shivering leaves away,
Again its dæmons far will fly,
When milder spirits rule the sky;
The moon of birds her horns will show,
The bough will bud, the fountain flow:
But, Metacom, thy second spring
No Weko-lis shall ever sing!
Once Pawkanawkut's warriors stood,
Thick as the columns of the wood;
On shores and isles, unconquered men
Called Massasoiet Father, then:—

The blasting wind with poisoned breath
Brought on its withered pinions death,
Ere bade the OWANNOX o'er the deep
Their castle-barks triumphant sweep:—
Past is the Autumn of our pride,
When every leaf with blood was died:—
And now dread Winter's troop alone
Shriek round our power and promise gone!
From earth when nations perish, ne'er
Again their leaflets shall appear.
The stranger, in the after time,
Weets not of glory's earlier clime!
Perchance, like yon dwarf firs that grow
Rooted in rocky cleft on high,
As things above, or joy or wo,
That frown against the beauteous sky,—
Of all our tribes, the heirs of want,
A feeble few our land may haunt;
The gloomy ghosts of dead renown
Awhile from sire to son go down;
And as with spectral visit say
That here the red men once had sway!

XXVIII.

" Veiling in gloom his awful face,
The Spirit smiles not on our race,
As once he smiled with beams of bliss,
Ere discord's snakes were heard to hiss.
One council fire the nations knew;
One ample roof o'er all was spread;
The stately tree beside it grew,
The skies of blue rose overhead.
Once on our wampum-belts, how fair
The stainless lines of peace were wrought,
And all the sacred symbols there
With wise and friendly meaning fraught!
Once circling far the glittering chain
Begirt the sea, the isles, the main;
The belt is broke; the chain is riven,
And we are left by angry heaven!
Fraught with our weal and with our wo,
The tide of fate runs deep and slow;
On to eternity it rides,
    Mysterious as the wave,

Where Huron disembogues its tides,
That slowly rises, slow subsides,
  As cycles find their grave.
Full low our country's best blood runs,
And few and feeble are her sons;
Will ye the desperate venture try,
And leave the dreary channel dry?

XXIX.

" Wild are the wolds and deep the woods
That girdle far our western floods:
There merrily the red-deer roam,
There may we fight ourselves a home!
Yet may *submission* purchase *peace*,"
" Cease," cried the furious SACHEM, " cease!"
For long had died the war-whoop's strain,
The warrior's fire was quenched again.
As the last moanings of the gale
Sigh out the tempest's sad farewell,
The whirlwind wakened by their lord
  In mournful murmurs died;

And thro' that melancholy horde
  Sunk all their wakened pride.

XXX.

" Traitor, enough! thy wish is given!
Go howl around the walls of heaven!
There's ample room, apostate! there;
Go thou that company to share
Of spectres vile, whom doom decreed
Proclaims the dastard traitor's meed.
For aye those guilty shadows speed
    Swift thro' that misty land,
On feverish chase, which end hath none,
Whose phantom game shall ne'er be won,
Till retribution shall be done;—
    Go, then, to join the band!
Seal with thy blood the covenant made,
When UNCAS first our rights betrayed.
The white man's arms are best employed,
Their recreant proselyte destroyed."

XXXI.

He said, and from beside him caught
The tube with deadly vengeance fraught;—
Then instant forth Ahauton stood,
(He too of the Mohegan blood,)
But short the raving Sachem broke
The words the intercessor spoke.
"By Sassacöus' honoured bones,
Where'er, untombed in sacred stones,
In the fierce Maquas clime they lie—
No more, or with him shalt thou die!"
Then on his friend the sentenced chief
Cast a last look intent and brief;
It bade Ahauton not to dare
The wolf's wild fangs within his lair,
But life for nobler vengeance bear.
Stern lowered the Wampanoägs round,
Subdued beneath their chieftain's frown;
Breathed to the doom of death no sound,
While Agamoun knelt calmly down,
Unblenched and firm; awhile his gaze
The horde, the earth, the heaven surveys,

As giving them his last good-bye :—
" Brothers ! behold a warrior die !
For kindred let the white men grieve ;
To those who love me, all I leave
Is the large legacy of hate !
True as the ball that drinks my blood,
Mohegan warriors shall make good
To METACOM and his the debt.
Escape be yours ;—but O ! if won,
  Beware !" he spoke no more,
For closely now the levelled gun
  Was placed his heart before.

XXXII.

A moment's pause intensely still,—
A quick, cold, deep and silent thrill,—
The steel gives fire,—the chieftain fell,—
The death-shot's sound his only knell,
And a low murmur's smothered tone
His parting requiem alone !

XXXIII.

" Take, Areskoui ! take thine own !"—
With voice subdued the Sachem said,—
" A braver offering never bled,
To thee in battle's gory bed !
And I could mourn the recreant thought
By which so dear a life was bought,
But that I may not waste a sigh,
On foul, infectious treachery.
Brothers, away ! not yet the foe
These our last haunts of safety know ;
Till better days, our watch-word be
Hope, vigilance and secresy."

XXXIV.

They raise the bleeding corse, and back
Hold to their dark retreat the track ;
With Metacom remains alone
The brave, the generous Annawon.
" Brother and friend,"—the Sachem cried,
" The only friend my fortunes know,

When all by kin, by love allied,
Are captive to the unpitying foe,—
Or unavenged, are journeying slow
To that far world where spirits go :—
O friend ! my trust is firm in thee,
As in his dream the initiate's faith ;
Calm is thy soul in victory,
And bold when comes the hour of scaith.
Yon trembling herd it is not meet
Should read our final purpose yet ;
Their courage is an old year's flame,
Polluted and unworth the name ;
Terror alone their hearts must sway—
For this the brave has bled to-day.
But I must fly—my native earth,—
My father's throne and council-hearth ;—
I of the peerless eagle race,
Must fly the hawk's unwonted chase,—
The insatiate hawk—who all will have,
Nor yields his victim even a grave !
Since childhood's earlier moons were dead,

When I forgot what things had been,
And claimed to rank with warrior men—
Of mortal foe I knew no dread.
Had nature made these limbs to quail
At danger's front, the whitemen ne'er
Had chilled them with the spells of fear ;—
For, in those hours when dreams prevail,—
When on the boy's bewildered eyes
The future's shadowy visions rise,
I learnt to fear nor wound nor fate
From those pale offspring of the east :—
This too oft sung the illumined priest,
When heaven he might interrogate,
Ere the Manittos' voices ceased.
This have I felt, when slaughter fell
Shrieked in my ear its murderous yell ;—
This in the kindling battle's mell,
In deathful stour was proven well ;—
This have my widowed fortunes found,
When all I love lie cold around ;—
When like a blasted trunk, alone,
Leaf, blossom, bud and scion gone,

I stand,—the fire, the axe defy,
And swift-consuming bolts on high.
It is not fear !—but o'er my heart
The shade of sorrow oft will fly ;—
And though from these fair scenes to part
Might ask the tribute of a sigh,—
That sigh, the last, the only one,
Becomes not MASSASOIET's son !

XXXV.

" But let this pass ;—by fraud or force,
Through Nipnet tribes we hold our course ;
YAMOYDEN to their broken bands
Yet dear, must through their northern lands
Make smooth our path. Thou say'st that he
Lists in Aquetnet's woods to hear
A bird, whose music is more dear
Than vengeance or than liberty.
A turtle dove he nurses there,
And shelters with a parent's care.
That nest must be despoiled ! the chief
Must share our common bond of grief !

And hear me, chieftain—ere our flight,
The last, the long-neglected rite,
Again must blaze in midnight gloom,
Prove if the spirits yet be dumb!
Since Areskoui sees no more,
Supine in heaven, his children's wo,
Evoking powers, our friends of yore,
The sacrifice of blood must pour,
And o'er their awful altars flow!"

XXXVI.

Here pause we for a while the song,
While they their counsels wild prolong,
Where many a troubled accent came,
Oft mingling with Yamoyden's name.

YAMOYDEN.

CANTO II.

YAMOYDEN.

CANTO SECOND.

Hail! sober Evening! thee the harassed brain
And aching heart with fond orisons greet:
The respite thou of toil; the balm of pain;
To thoughtful mind the hour for musing meet:
'Tis then the sage, from forth his lone retreat,
The rolling universe around espies;
'Tis then the bard may hold communion sweet
With lovely shapes, unkenned by grosser eyes,
And quick perception comes of finer mysteries.

The silent hour of bliss! when in the west
Her argent cresset lights the star of love:—
The spiritual hour! when creatures blest
Unseen return o'er former haunts to rove;
While sleep his shadowy mantle spreads above,
Sleep, brother of forgetfulness and death,
Round well-known couch, with noiseless tread they rove,
In tones of heavenly music comfort breathe,
And tell what weal or bale shall chance the moon beneath.

Hour of devotion! like a distant sea,
The world's loud voices faintly murmuring die;
Responsive to the spheral harmony,
While grateful hymns are borne from earth on high.
O! who can gaze on yon unsullied sky,
And not grow purer from the heavenward view!
As those, the Virgin Mother's meek, full eye,
Who met, if uninspirèd lore be true,
Felt a new birth within, and sin no longer knew.

Let others hail the oriflamme of morn,
O'er kindling hills unfurled with gorgeous dies!
O mild, blue Evening! still to thee I turn,
With holier thought, and with undazzled eyes;—
Where wealth and power with glare and splendour rise,
Let fools and slaves disgustful incense burn!
Still Memory's moonlight lustre let me prize;
The great, the good, whose course is o'er, discern,
And, from their glories past, time's mighty lessons learn!

I.

The sun is sinking from the sky
In calm and cloudless majesty;
And cooler hours, with gentle sway,
Succeed the fiery heat of day.

Forest and shore and rippling tide
Confess the evening's influence wide,
Seen lovelier in that fading light,
That heralds the approaching night;—
That magic colouring nature throws,
To deck her beautiful repose;—
When floating on the breeze of even,
Long clouds of purple streak the heaven,
With brighter tints of glory blending,
And darker hues of night descending.
While hastening to its shady rest
Each weary songster seeks its nest,
Chanting a last, a farewell lay,
As gloomier falls the parting day.

II.

Broad Narraganset's bosom blue
Has shone with every varying hue;
The mystic alchemy of even
Its rich delusions all has given.
The silvery sheet unbounded spread,
First melting from the waters fled;

Next the wide path of beaten gold
Flashing with fiery sparkles rolled ;—
As all its gorgeous glories died,
An amber tinge blushed o'er the tide ;
Faint and more faint, as more remote,
The lessening ripples peaceful float ;
And now, one ruby line alone
Trembles, is paler, and is gone,—
And from the blue wave fades away
The last life-tint of dying day !
In darkness veiled, was seen no more
Connanicut's extended shore ;
Each little isle with bosom green,
Descending mists impervious screen ;
One gloomy shade o'er all the woods
Of forest-fringed Aquetnet broods ;
Where solemn oak was seen before
Beside the rival sycamore,
Or pine and cedar lined the height,
All in one livery brown were dight.

III.

But lo! with orb serene on high,
The round moon climbs the eastern sky;
The stars all quench their feebler rays
Before her universal blaze.
Round moon! how sweetly dost thou smile,
Above that green reposing isle,—
Soft cradled in the illumined bay,
Where from its bank the shadows seem
Melting in filmy light away.
Far does thy tempered lustre stream,
Chequering the tufted groves on high,
While glens in gloom beneath them lie.
Oft sheeted with the ghostly beam,
Mid the thick forest's mass of shade,
The shingled roof is gleaming white,
Where labour, in the cultured glade,
Has all the wild a garden made.
And there with silvery tassels bright
The serried maize is waving slow,
While fitful shadows come and go,

Swift o'er its undulating seas,
As gently breathes the evening breeze.

IV.

Solemn it is, in greenwoods deep,
That magic light o'er nature's sleep;
Where in long ranks the pillars gray
Aloft their mingling structures bear,—
Mingling, in gloom or tracery fair,
Where find the unbroken beams their way,—
Or through close trellis flickering stray,
While sheeny leaflets here and there
Flutter, with momentary glow.
'Tis wayward life revealed below,
With chequered gleams of joy and wo!
And those, pure realms above that shine,
So chaste, so vivid, so divine,
Are the sole type that heaven has shown
Of those more lovely realms, its own!

V.

There is no sound amid the trees,
Save the faint brush of rustling breeze;

Save insect sentinels, that still
Prolong their constant larum shrill,
And answer all, from tree to tree,
With one monotonous revelry.
And at this hushed and solemn hour,
As gradual thro' the tangled woods,
Mystery usurps her wonted power,
The spirit of the solitudes,—
Musing upon her lonely state,
As plains the dove her absent mate,
Sad NORA sits, and mournfully
Sings her dear infant's lullaby.

VI.

Sorrow had been her lot. She loved,
As few have loved of earthly frame;
And misery but too well had proved
Her anguished heart was still the same.
Ere Areskoui's wild alarms
Called all the red men forth to arms,
A Nipnet chieftain wooed and won
Her virgin love; and when begun

The desolating strife, his care
Long screened her from the quest of war.
Night closed on PHILIP's victor day,
And hurrying in the desperate fray,
The Nipnet chieftain with his bride
Were borne near Haup's beleaguered side.
A home he found, that none could know,
So deemed the chief,—or friend, or foe;
He placed her in that island grove,
With one dear pledge of mutual love.
Deep in the forest's bosom green,
  Their cot embowered arose;
Enveloped in its woven screen,
  And wrapt in calm repose.
The fairy humming-bird could scarce
Amid the boughs its entrance pierce;
And practised Indian's hunter eye
Would fail to trace its mystery.
One eye alone its labyrinth knew,
One only heart to NORA true.
Here while her vigil sad she keeps,
And lists in vain YAMOYDEN's steps,

Her weeping babe she hushed to rest,
And lulled upon her heaving breast,
Or wove a passing strain to cheat
The tedious hours with music sweet.

VII.

" Sleep, child of my love! be thy slumber as light
  As the red bird's that nestles secure on the spray;
Be the visions that visit thee fairy and bright
  As the dew drops that sparkle around with the ray!
O soft flows the breath from thine innocent breast;
  In the wild wood, sleep cradles in roses thy head;
But her who protects thee, a wanderer unblest,
  He forsakes, or surrounds with his phantoms of
      dread.
I fear for thy father! why stays he so long
  On the shores where the wife of the giant was
      thrown,
And the sailor oft lingered to hearken her song,
  So sad o'er the wave, e'er she hardened to stone.
He skims the blue tide in his birchen canoe,
  Where the foe in the moon-beams his path may
      descry;

The ball to its scope may speed rapid and true,
  And lost in the wave be thy father's death cry!
The POWER that is round us,—whose presence is near,
  In the gloom and the solitude felt by the soul,
Protect that frail bark in its lonely career,
  And shield *thee*, when roughly life's billows shall roll."

VIII.

The noise of parting boughs was heard,
Within the wood a footstep stirred;
The partner of her griefs appears,
To kiss away her falling tears.
"And oh!" YAMOYDEN said, "that thou
This sad reverse of life should'st know!
Wretch that I was, with hand unblest,
To snatch this nursling from her nest,
And bear her with me darkly on,
Through horror's tide and misery's moan!
Alone, though wild the tempest raved,
The roar, the flash, I might have braved;—

But thou, so young, so wondrous fair,
A wanderer's restless lot to share—"
"Mourn not for me," she calm replied,
"With thee, the worst I can abide;
And hope and joy are present here
Mid tenfold gloom, if thou art near.
And in the hour of darkest ill,
There is a hope, a refuge still—
Lift we our thoughts, our prayers on high,—
There's comfort in eternity!"

IX.

In rapt delight the chieftain gazed,—
Her pale, fair brow was upward raised;
In her blue eye devotion shone,
With that mild radiance, all its own,
Such as might mark, with purer light,
O'er heaven a passing seraph's flight.
"Nora, thou cam'st, mid dreary strife,
To bless and cheer a wayward life;—
O! thou wast borne upon my sight,
In blessedness and beauty given,

Of all good tidings omen fair;
As floating thro' the azure air,
The Wakon bird descends from heaven,
Poised on his fleet and equal wings,
And from his glittering train far flings,
Marking his pathway from above,
The rainbow hues of peace and love!
Not vain hath been thy care to teach
The great, good Spirit's belovëd speech;
And not in vain thy words have shown
The prophet who from high came down,
The Priest and Offering. I have sought
His ear, with prayers thy lips have taught,
When clouds above were deep and dread,
And brightness seemed around them shed,
Till, like yon snow-wreaths of the sky,
They passed in fading lustre by.
When lone I crost the silent wave,
While its soft light the moon-beam gave,
And all above, and all below,
Was kindling with the heavenly glow,
My heart was full of prayer; and then,

Methought thy hopes would not be vain.
I felt the Comforter appear,
And every doubt and every fear
Depart; the cheering presence stole
With sweeter influence on my soul,
Than the mild breeze around my frame,
That o'er the tranquil waters came.
Oh! on the bare and wintry ground,
When utter darkness reigned around,
Oft have I watched the morning star
Break thro' the eastern mists afar;
But never yet upon my view
It came in such immortal hue,
As that glad beam of hope that stole
Above the darkness of my soul."

X.

Entranced in sudden bliss they sate,
Forgetful of the storms of fate;
With thoughts by favoured minstrels sung
    Amid their happiest numbers,
While o'er her child the mother hung
    And marked its innocent slumbers;

Or met Yamoyden's kindling gaze
Where mingling love and rapture blaze :—
The hawk's wild scream the silence broke,
Again the sense of pain awoke.

XI.

" And I must go," the chieftain cried,
" To join the children of despair ;—
The eagle may fly to his mountain side,
And the panther from toils and death may hide,
In his wood-circled lair ;
But they, the lords of earth and sea,
May to no home of refuge flee !"
" O why forsake thy child and me ?
Thou art not summoned there—
Where thou, a Christian, may'st again
Thy hands with Christian slaughter stain !"
" Nora, if recreant thought were here,
For us what hope, what home is near ?
The base Mohegan's hand would sink
The treacherous axe within my brain ;—
I have not learnt from death to shrink,

Yet keener far than torture's pain,
Or the vile foe's exulting strain,
It were, upon thy woes to think;—
For thou, thy kinsmen's scorn, would'st live
Unpitied and alone to grieve.
And this my boy—it cannot be!
I would, when I am dead, that he
Should be the Indian's friend,—should bear
Glad tidings to our tribes dispersed;
Should plant the vine and olive there,
And deep beneath the foliage fair
Bury the tomahawk accurst.
But friend and foe alike would shun
The traitor's child, the coward's son!
They shall not say that when the fire
Circled the hunted herd, his sire
Wept like the roebuck when he flies,
And died as warrior never dies.

XII.

"I sought Seaconet's queen to try
Her faith once plighted to the brave;

But she, in sore extremity,
Received the axe the white men gave;
Her tribe has joined their battle cry;
Alone, unaided, we must fly,
Break through our toils, the hunter bands,
To find a home in happier lands.
O haply yet, our dangers past,
Some blest retreat may rise at last.
Yet may we find some lovely plain,
A world within itself our own;
Encircled by a mountain chain,
Whose crests eternal forests crown;
While through the midst, serene and slow,
A gently winding stream shall flow.
Those woods, whose undisputed sway
The buskined hunter genii keep,—
That stream, whose banks, in guileful play,
Behold the wily red fox leap,
To snare the sportive birds, whose fate
Those treacherous gambols proves too late,—
Those scenes no war-whoop shall assail:
The vines untrod shall clothe the vale,

Thick mantling with their cheerful hues
And clustering with their purple store;
From the full bark the honeyed juice
Its gushing treasures round shall pour;
There melons with their varying die
Shall bask beneath a milder sky;
The plumed maize, with shapely blade,
Shall stand like marshalled host arrayed.
Oh! there the tranquil hours shall flow,
Calm as the glassy wave below;
Remembrance of past griefs shall cease
In the sweet bosom of that peace,
Yielding rich streams of comfort blest,
Like balmy fountains of the west,
Which Spirits gift by healing charm,
With unction meet for every harm!"

XIII.

"Yamoyden, 'tis a blissful dream,—
A glimpse of heaven thro' thunder-clouds;
Despair forbids such light to beam
O'er the deep gloom our fate that shrouds.

Dark is the lord whose desperate cause
Thou followest; yet for reason pause;
Pause, ere that heart of guilt and guile
Entrap thee in its latest wile!"
"Fear not; his wasted power forbids
The secret hope of hostile deeds.
Yet if Revenge the spirit be
That holds the SACHEM company,
How shall his foes the outlaw blame,
Or marvel whence the dæmon came?
Can he forget, while heaves his breath,
An outraged brother's captive death?
Can he forget the lurid light
Of Narraganset's bloody night?
The forests broad his fathers swayed,
O'errun beneath the oppressor's tread;—
The bones that bleach in every fen,
The perished race of warrior men;—
The limbs once cast in freedom's mould,
Fettered in slavery's iron hold;—
The wanderer of the lonely place
Waylaid, and tortured to confess;—

His kindred slain, or captive led;—
A price upon his homeless head;—
O! his are wrongs that but with death
From burning memory can depart;
All the pure waters of thy faith
Could wash them ne'er from human heart!

XIV.

" Farewell! the sound is as the wail
That rises o'er the closing grave!
While yet the shades of night prevail,
My boat must cross once more the wave.
I go to speed our brethren's flight,
And with the morrow's closing light,
Return to bear thee hence, and far
For ever fly from sounds of war."
" Farewell! I will not weep;"—she said,
Tho' stealing from its liquid bed
There fell the unbidden tear;—
I will not weep;—a warrior's wife
Must learn the moods of wayward life,
Nor know the form of fear.

There is a chill my bosom o'er,
Which sadly says, we meet no more.
But let it pass ;—farewell ! and God
Preserve thee, on the path of blood !"

XV.

Mute was their last embrace, and sad,
Forth fared the chief thro' forest shade ;
And still, like statue of despair
His lonely bride stood fixëd there,
Gazing entranced on vacant air ;
Sense, feeling, wrapt in this alone,
The cherished theme of love was gone.
One throb remained ;—the spell it broke,
When her unconscious infant woke ;
Maternal cares recalled her thought,
And soothed her labouring breast o'erfraught,
While thus again her accents flow
In deep accordance with her wo.

XVI.

1.

"They say that afar in the land of the west,
Where the bright golden sun sinks in glory to rest,
Mid fens where the hunter ne'er ventured to tread,
A fair lake unruffled and sparkling is spread;
Where, lost in his course, the rapt Indian discovers,
In distance seen dimly, the green isle of lovers.

2.

"There verdure fades never; immortal in bloom,
Soft waves the magnolia its groves of perfume;
And low bends the branch with rich fruitage deprest,
All glowing like gems in the crowns of the east;
There the bright eye of Nature, in mild glory hovers:
'Tis the land of the sunbeam,—the green isle of lovers!

3.

"Sweet strains wildly float on the breezes that kiss
The calm-flowing lake round that region of bliss;
Where, wreathing their garlands of amaranth, fair choirs
Glad measures still weave to the sound that inspires

The dance and the revel, mid forests that cover
On high with their shade the green isle of the lover.

4.

"But fierce as the snake with his eyeballs of fire,
When his scales are all brilliant and glowing with
ire,
Are the warriors to all, save the maids of their isle,
Whose law is their will, and whose life is their smile;
From beauty there valour and strength are not
rovers,
And peace reigns supreme in the green isle of lovers.

5.

"And he who has sought to set foot on its shore,
In mazes perplext, has beheld it no more;
It fleets on the vision, deluding the view,
Its banks still retire as the hunters pursue;
O! who in this vain world of wo shall discover,
The home undisturbed, the green isle of the lover!"

XVII.

What sound was that, so wildly sad,
As by prophetic spirit made?

So sudden, mid the silence deep,
Breaking on nature's death-like sleep?
'Twas but the lonely We-ko-lis,
Who oft, at such an hour as this,
Had from the woven boughs around
Prolonged her melancholy sound.
But now she perched upon the roof,
And from her wonted spray aloof,
In interrupted notes of wo
Poured forth her solemn music slow,
With tremulous and mournful note,
Now nearer heard, and now remote.—
And she had heard an Indian tell,
Such sound foreboded sudden bale.
It was the soul of a lovelorn maid,
Who mourned her warrior slain, he said.—
But little faith, I ween, had she,
A Christian bred, in augury;
Yet strove, alternate fear and shame,
Till all the woman's terrors came.

XVIII.

There is a trampling in the wood;—
The mat, the cabin's entrance rude,
Shakes;—it was no dream of fear,—
Behold an Indian's face appear;—
He stands within the cot,—and three
Come scowling in his company.
Ask not what terrors o'er her past,
As fixed as stood the patriarch's wife,
When the forbidden glance she cast,
And lightning rooted her aghast,
Leaving a mock of life,—
Gazing she sate, in silent dread,
Till sight was gone, and thought was dead:
Yet close and closer still, she prest
The sleeping infant on her breast;
A mother's instinct quick was left,
Of other sign of life bereft.

XIX.

But when she felt an iron grasp
Tearing that infant from her clasp,

Her piercing scream the forest rent,
And all despair's high strength was sent
Gathering around her heart;
" O mercy, Jesus! save my child!"
She cried in tones so sadly wild,
The WAMPANOAG, fierce and bold,
Shrunk from his purpose, and his hold
Relaxed with sudden start.
Her spoiler's dusky brow she scanned,—
Yet struggling from his ruthless hand
Her wailing child to tear,—
As one would mark the madman's eye,
When a fearful precipice was nigh,
And he had grasped him there.
She met his glances, stern and keen,
Such might the hungry wolf's have been,—
Whose spoils now swathed him round;—
And in his front all bare and bleak,
And in his high, scar-riven cheek,
No line of mercy found.
A rapid look surveyed the rest;—
In vain to them despair may cling!

Ah! sooner mantling verdure blest
On the bald thundercliff shall spring!

XX.

The mother from her child is torn,—
A cry that rent her heart forlorn,
Their murderous triumph told;
Then kind oblivion came to save
From madness; dark, as is the grave,
Dreamless and void and cold.
One bears her senseless in his arms,
Another stills the babe's alarms;
Then through the forest's tangled way,
Swift and straight, toward the bay
Their path the Indians hold.
Each stepping where the first had gone,
'Twas but as the mark of one.
So noiseless was their cautious tread,
The wakeful squirrel overhead
Knew not that aught beneath him sped.
No bough recoiled as on they broke,
Scarce rustling leaf their impress spoke.

XXI.

From the first blush who judges man,
Must ill his Maker's image scan:
The traveller in the boundless lands,
Where the fair west its stores expands,
Oft marks, with cheerful green unblent,
High piled to heaven the bleak ascent,
As scathed and blasted by the fire,
That fell from the Almighty's ire.
But as along the vale he sweeps,
More gently swell the fir-clad steeps,
Till all the sunny mountain rise,
With golden crown amid the skies.
Not the swarth skin, nor rude address
Bespeak the bosom's dreariness;—
Happy, if thus the evil brain
Bore stampt the outward curse of Cain!

XXII.

Slowly from Nora's wandering soul,
Oblivion's mists of midnight roll,

And, as she woke, to view again
Uncertain horror's spectral train,
Dashing waves were murmuring near,
Rode the bright moon high and clear:
The plunderers crost a shelving glade;
Around the forest's mass of shade
Rose darkling; and before, the bay
Was quivering with the silver ray.
Dim memory rose; an Indian eye
Watched its first dawning earnestly.
Strange was the face that, frank and bold,
Spoke a heart cast in gentler mould.
He bore the waking lady up
And lingered last of all the group;
Nor e'er at superstition's shrine,
Did votary mark the fire divine,
When wavering in its golden vase,
With feeling more intense,
Than o'er her wan and death-like face,—
Like morning blushing o'er the snow,—
The warrior watched the beaming glow
Of lost intelligence.

XXIII.

He pointed, where his comrade bore
Her infant in his arms, before.
His gaze with melting ruth was fraught,
And that uncertain peril taught
A language to his look:
Of needful silence in that hour,
Of rescue near from saviour power
And faithful aid it spoke.
But still they sped toward the wave,
And he whose glance had sworn to save,
Yet often eyed the circling wood
Where only gloom and mystery brood.
The rippling tides, the insects shrill,
At times the plaining whip-poor-will,
In melancholy concord wake;
But other sound was none, to break
The wild suspense of hope and fear;
There was no sign of rescue near.
Fair shone the moon; but there gleamed no ray
Of hope in her calm and pearly way;

Bright rolled the expanding floods below,
But there shone no promise in their flow;
The hues serene of nature's rest
But agonized her anxious breast.

XXIV.

Nearer and nearer to the shore,
Their prize the hurrying party bore;—
The bank is gained; its brake amid,
Their light canoe was closely hid.
While cautious its descent they guide,
To the calm bosom of the tide,
Their comrade, lingering yet above,
Gazed anxiously around to prove
His silent promise true;—
But not a sound is heard, nor sign
Is there of aid; the giant pine
Its gloomy limbs unmoving bears,
And still the silent forest wears
Its sad and solemn hue.

XXV.

'Tis launched,—they beckon him to haste;
One glance he threw, and hope has past,
No more could NORA brook to wait,
In passiveness, uncertain fate.
She shrieked,—far rung the loud alarm,—
And as she struggled from his arm
To break, whose faint resistance made
A moment's brief delay,
An Indian leapt to lend his aid;
But, ere he touched the trembling maid,
Even in his middle way,—
Loud from the wood a gunshot rung,
Straight from earth the NIPNET sprung,
Then, with but one mortal pain,
Dead he sunk upon the plain.
Again, again the volleys pour,
And NORA saw and heard no more.

XXVI.

She woke; the ground was wet with blood,—
Her Indian saviour o'er her stood;

Around her she discovered then,
The faces of her countrymen.
"Where is my child?" they answer not;—
Her dusky guardian's eye she sought;—
O'er his high cheek of rugged mould,
The moon-beam glistened, clear and cold;
A crystal tear was starting bright,
And glittering with the pale, pure light;—
"Where is my child? in mercy, say?"
He pointed to the expanding bay;—
There was no speck on its azure sheet,
No trace in the waters smooth and fleet,—
As if furrowing keel had ploughed them never,—
And she knew her child was gone for ever.

YAMOYDEN.

CANTO III.

YAMOYDEN.

CANTO THIRD.

Bright as the bird whom Indian legends sing,
Whose glance was lightning, and whose eye was flame,
The deep-voiced thunder trembling in his wing,
When from the ocean earth emerging came;—
Fair freedom soars with wing and glance the same,
And calls, from depths profound and cheerless waste,
The quickening spark that fires the burning frame,
Glows deathless in the patriot's ardent breast,
While loud the thunders speak, where lie her sons opprest.

O who hath ever from her buoyant air
Drank vigorous life beneath her wings outspread,
And would not that the scenes of nature fair
Lay rather like the desert seared and dead,—

Than see the spirit that inspired them fled,
Quenched the bright lightnings of her awful eye;
Hope, valour, crushed beneath oppression's tread,
And o'er the darkening scene of death descry
How stern destruction holds her drear ascendency.

Hearts that loved freedom came, away to tear
From fellow men, that birthright which they blest;
And they, to whom religion's cause was dear,
Fanned the unholy passion in their breast;—
The persecuted sought on the opprest
To trample;—bared the exterminating sword,
Above their victim's last, defenceless rest;
Yea, self-deluded, loud their cries they pour'd
For aid, to HIM, the God of peace, whom they adored.

I.

While hot pursuit a moment failed,
The victor host their council held;—
Tho' boastful hope had vaunted sure
Their victim and his band secure,
Yet varied tale and rumours dark
Misled them from their destined mark;
And on Pocasset's winding shore,
Awhile they gave the hunting o'er,

And on the island now they rest,
Which blooms o'er ocean's placid breast,
In its bright emerald livery drest,
  The garden of the deep;
They heeded not its verdant bowers,
Its peaceful groves and myriad flowers,—
Snatching a few uncertain hours,
  Their council stern to keep.
But few were met;—their scouts afar
Pursued the scent of failing war;
While here in anxious doubt they stay,
Thus rose the supplicating lay.

II.

War Hymn.

1.

O Thou! for whom in the heavens high
Seraphim embattled fly!
Before us be thy banner spread
Like the pillar of fire which thy people led!

2.

Almighty Conqueror! to thee we cry;—
Gird thy bright falchion on thy thigh;

Let all creation's trembling arch
Proclaim our God's victorious march!

3.

King of all kings! to thee belongs
To inspire our weak and mortal songs;
Hear the strains thy Spirit taught
Through HIM that our ransom from death hath
bought.

4.

May we break on the foe, to blaspheme thee who
dared,
With the sword of thy righteousness, whetted and
bared,
As burst, when their fountains are broken, the
floods,
As the storm when it tears up the pride of the
woods.

5.

They shall fade like the smoke which is lost in the
air,
They shall melt from thy wrath when its fury shall
glare;

Unblenched shall we track them, through wild
flowing war,
By the light of our battle, thy conquering star!

III.

Ceased the deep strain. On every brow
Sat exultation's crimson glow;
And every bosom beat, as high
Swelled the loud anthem to the sky.
They felt, as if on promised land,
Like Israel's guided host,
They followed heaven's directing hand,
To every isle and coast;
They felt as if his word had bade
Their ranks unsheath the glittering blade,
Whose high command to JOSHUA given
Led Jacob to his earthly heaven!
No throb was there of pity's mood,
For native of the solitude;
Doomed to the carnage of the sword
They deemed the country and its lord;

And bigot zeal, to bosoms brave,
The callous thirst of slaughter gave.
—On each flushed cheek, and glistening eye,
The glowing fever revelled high;
While fancy's fixed—unbounded gaze,
Almost beheld the Godhead's blaze;
As upwards, in extatic trance,
Beamed on the azure heaven their glance.
Awhile they stood. No word was spoken—
Deep was that silence, and unbroken—
Even the dark water's hollow roar
Was hushed upon the rocky shore,—
The wood-wind's music clear and shrill
Amid that solemn pause was still;—
Till, with one sudden burst again
Arose the animating strain.

IV.

Hymn.

1.

Lift up thy banner, Lord, afar,
  Arrayed in robes of dazzling light!

Arise, O Conqueror, to the war,
In all the glories of thy might!

2.

For who is God, save Thou, and where
Shall man find safety but in Thee?
Thy strength shall aid, thy kindly care
Preserve in blest security.

3.

The God of armies on our side
Hath waged his warfare, and o'ercome;
And he shall be our stay and guide,
Our hope, our refuge, and our home.

4.

High as the heavens, to God again
Lift then the song that tells his praise;
And earth prolong the solemn strain,
And angels tune their golden lays.

V.

As dies, far heard along the shore,
The ocean's deep and sullen roar;

As down the mountain's rugged brow
The failing thunder's echoes flow;
At first, in cadence wild and strong,
The notes profound their voice prolong,
Till, rolling far, they part and die,
Tho' still unquenched their majesty;—
So hushed the strain;—so sunk away
The Christian warrior's ardent lay;
So far the mighty echoes flow.
The Indian, in his light canoe,
E'en at Seaconet's troubled wave,

Felt terror shake his bosom brave;
And shrunk, within his fragile boat,
To hear that long re-echoed note:—
Omen of sorrow, deep and dire,
Of rending sword,—of wasting fire,—
Of hopes destroyed,—of bosoms torn,—
Of exile, cheerless and forlorn,—
Of power extinct, and glory gone,—
And his last boon—despair alone.

VI.

Fair breathes the morn; but not for him
Its floods of golden glory swim,
  The outcast wretch forlorn;
There is no sunrise in his breast—
He turns him from the kindling east,
And, like some wandering ghost unblest,
  Flies the sweet breath of morn.
The sea-gull skims along the waves,
Its snow-white bosom gladly laves;
The eagle cleaves the rack, and sails
High o'er the clouds and nether gales;
The red deer heaves his antlers high,
Bounding in "tameless transport by;"—
But what with them to do hath he?
They, like the elements, are FREE!
And thoughts, than death more dread and deep,
Across his mental vision sweep,
While only lives the soul for pain,
Like vulture tyring on the brain.*

* The seven first verses of this canto were transcribed by their author, but a few weeks before his death; and have been printed exactly after his manuscript.

VII.

Yet to the camp no tidings come
Where Philip and his followers roam;
And, while the scent was cold,
The English band that tracked his way,
Beneath broad oaks embowering lay,
And varying converse hold.
Small space between them, and the rout
Of Indians who had joined the shout,
That hung on Philip's flight:
Mohegans and Seaconets too,
A motley band, in numbers few,
Were gathered for the fight.

VIII.

Amid the Christian corps there stood
A gray old man; the book of God
Was in his hand; with holy verse
That spoke the ancient heathen's curse,
He blest the murders they had done,
And called on heaven the work to crown.

As o'er the past their converse turned,
His eye with inspiration burned,
While thus his speech began to flow
O'er earlier scenes of toils and wo.

IX.

"Nor lure of conquest's meteor beam,
Nor dazzling mines of fancy's dream,
Nor wild adventure's love to roam,
Brought from their father's ancient home,
Mid labours, deaths, and dangers tost,
O'er the wide sea the pilgrim host.
They braved the battle and the flood,
To worship here their fathers' GOD.
With shreds of papal vesture tied
To flaunting robes of princely pride,
In formal state, on sumptuous throne,
Daughter of her of Babylon,
Sat bigotry. Her chilling breath
To fires of heavenly warmth was death;
Her iron sceptre England swayed,
Religion withering in its shade.

The shepherd might not kneel to call
On Him, the common sire of all,
Unless his lips, with harsh constraint,
Were tuned to accents cold and faint:
For man's devices had o'erwrought
The volume by a Saviour bought;
And clogged devotion's soaring wing
That up to heaven should instant spring,
With phrases set, that bore no part
In the warm service of the heart.
But why recount their sorrows past,
From the first martyr to the last?
Or pope's or bishop's bigot zeal,
Alike their hate of Christian weal;
Or torture's pangs and faggot's flame,
Or fines and exile, 'twas the same,
Same Antichrist, whom prophets old
With sad announcing voice foretold!

X.

" Such were the wrongs that cried to heaven—
What time shall see those wrongs forgiven!

O England! from thine earliest age,
Land of the warrior and the sage!
Eyrie of freedom, reared on rocks
That frown o'er ancient ocean's shocks!
Cradle of art! religion's fane,
Whose incense ne'er aspired in vain!
Temple of laws that shall not die,
When brass and marble crumbled lie!
Parent of bards whose harps rehearse
Immortal deeds in deathless verse!
O England! can thy pride forget
Thy soil with martyrs' blood is wet?
Bethink thee,—like the plagues which sleep
In earth's dark bosom buried deep,
As the poor savage deems,—that o'er
Thine head, the vials yet in store,
Vials of righteous wrath must pour!

XI.

"Strong was the love to heaven which bare
From their dear homes and altars far,

The old, the young, the wise, the brave,
The rich, the noble and the fair,
And led them, o'er the mighty wave,
Uncertain peril's front to dare.
Strong was their love; and strong the Power
Whose red right arm, in danger's hour,
Was bared on high their path to show,
Through changeful scenes of weal and wo;
By signs and wonders, as of old,
When Israel journeyed through the waste,
Was its mysterious guidance told;
Though lightnings flashed, and thunders rolled,
The sunbeam glorious smiled at last.

XII.

"How oft the storm their barks delayed,
How oft their prows they turned dismayed;
How oft his wings above their head
The death-announcing angel spread;
While the chill pestilential gale
Sung in the shrouds and shrinking sail!

They came; upon the soil they trod,
Where they might worship Nature's God;—
But not, as erst from Pisgah's height,
Burst on the Patriarch's aching sight
The promised realms of life and light,
Rose on their view the land they sought,
By exile, want, and misery bought.

XIII.

"Blazing o'er heaven with sickly flame,
A meteor fierce their herald came;
Plagues filled with death the tainted air,
To yield the Pilgrims entrance there.
A golgotha of skulls was spread
O'er all the land beneath their tread:—
For backward flew the savage race,
To give the new intruders space;
Expected now their wilds among,
Foretold by captive's prophet tongue.
In dismal depths of swampy dell
Their Powahs met with purpose fell,—

With haggard eye, and howls of ire,
They called on famine, sword, and fire,
To fill the air with Christian groans,
And whiten earth with Christian bones.

XIV.

" God heard their blasphemy. Though not
By spells of theirs was ruin wrought,
For wisest ends, from man concealed,
The Indian curse was half fulfilled.
Gaunt famine came ;—with ghastly train
Of all the screaming fiends of pain,
He stalked o'er forest, hill and plain ;
On herb and tree his mildew dealt,
And man and beast the syroc felt.
Long fed they on the withering roots,
Wild berries and the forest fruits ;
With what the barren ocean flung,
From its vast womb their rocks among ;
Until their numbers grow too weak,
Such scanty sustenance to seek.
Then fled the rose from beauty's cheek ;

Then the last spark cold age that fired,
Gleamed in its socket and expired;
Then youth unripe its stem forsook;
Untimely blasts the sapling shook;
Then manhood's sterner sinews bowed;
Till death sat scowling o'er the crowd—
None left to lay, with pious pains,
In decent earth their cold remains.—
The heaven was brass above their head;
The earth was iron 'neath their tread;—
Then from its surface cracked and dry,
Egypt's worst pests their fears espy;
Crawled forth the myriad insect host,
With shrilly wings o'er all the coast;
The coming plagues their swarms declared,
Disease destroyed whom death had spared.
Sore were their trials; oft their toil
Was vainly spent on sterile soil;
Oft blazed their roofs with raging flame;
And oft the fierce tornado came,
And in its whelming fury ran
O'er all the works of God and man:

The tall pine like a wand it broke,
Plucked from its roots the giant oak,
Made all its mighty fibres writhe,
And whirled and wound it like a withe.

XV.

"Yet mark the all-preserving care,—
When helpless, faint, and sick they were,
And when the heathen might have trod
In dust and death the church of God,
A mortal terror o'er them came,
Withheld the sword and wasting flame;
And dread and reverence like a spell
On their unholy purpose fell.

XVI.

"Such were their changeful woes for years
Of toils and doubts, and hopes and fears.
Yet still before the freshening gale
New Pilgrims bade their canvass swell;
And he who whilome walked the sea,
The turbid waves of Galilee,

Lit the vast deep with heavenly ray,
And bade the waters yield them way;
Till in the wilderness arose
His church triumphant o'er her foes.
O'er heathen rage, and lips profane,
That mocked the sufferers' mortal pain,
When in their agonies they cried
On CHRIST to save their souls, and died;—
O'er daring sin, that strove to rear
The shrine of Dagon, even here;—
O'er damning error's secret wiles,
Prolific schism's delusive toils;—
O'er pagan and apostate foes,
The church of God triumphant rose.
Till now, o'er wilds where murder swayed,
Her branches cast their sacred shade,
Springing with instant growth to heaven,
Like the blest gourd to JONAH given.
Wo to the worm, whate'er it be,
Whose tooth corrodes that goodly tree!
If e'er the thirst for novel lore,
Half learnt pretension's shallow store,

Or foul design, with secret blow
To lay the goodly structure low,
Corrupt the sacred faith we own,
Or pluck from CHRIST the GODHEAD'S crown,
Then shall the Indian curse yet fall
In whelming fury on them all!
Ruin and havoc shall again
Destroy their homes and blight their plain;
To after ages shall they be
A proverb for their infamy!

XVII.

" The hour is come; the pagan host
Scattered, dissolves like morning frost.
The hour is come, when we shall tread
In dust the writhing serpent's head.
What mercy shall to him be shown
Who weds eternal hate alone?
Revenge his God—to murder led,
For this he woos e'en Christian aid;
When wreaked his wrath, he turns to dart
His sting into his patron's heart.

For this, on Moloch's streaming pyre,
He gives his children to the fire.
For this in torture he will die,
Smiling through all his agony;
Till, in its horrid transport lost,
To Tophet flies the howling ghost!
Thus saith the Lord—fear not their spite,
The outcast heathen's power to harm;
Against my people, in my sight,
They shall not raise the murderous arm.
His works in latter days proclaim
From age to age his power the same;
Even as of old when JOSHUA's word
The lights of heaven obedient heard;
O'er Gibeon's towers the lingering ray
Prolonged the unwonted blaze of day;
While hung the moon with crescent pale,
O'er Ajalon's undarkened vale."

XVIII.

Thus ran the preacher's theme; and long
Dwelt on his words the listening throng;

Recounting portents far and near
On rumour's gales inconstant driven,
Whence superstition's greedy ear
Drank in the immediate voice of heaven.
They talked of that polluted night
That saw the heathen's damning rite;
By God forsaken, when their spell
Conjured in aid the Prince of Hell:
When groans of tortured martyrs blended
With yells of furious joy ascended;
When, while the sacrifice was screaming,
The hot, baked earth was wet and steaming,
As drop by drop it caught the blood
Of saints, whose latest prayer to God
  In blasphemy was drowned.
Since then the savage crest was bowed,
Sunk was their spirit stern and proud,
Nor more was heard their war-cry loud,
  Through echoing groves to sound.
But judgment, with destruction fraught,
Hung o'er their heads, where'er they sought
  Escape from tempests round,

As broke the clouds of thunder o'er
The routed Amorites of yore.
Then talked they of the sign beheld
  By their advancing troop,
When through their borders first was yelled
  The death-announcing whoop;
When at the midnight's ghostly noon,
A crimson scar deformed the moon:
Like Indian scalp the shape it had;
And, while they gazed, the planet bright
Plunged into earth's o'erwhelming shade,
And veiled her silver orb in night.
From thence with awe had holy lips
Presaged the foe's more dark eclipse.
Nor this alone portended war;
Through the clear æther heard afar,
Strange sounds were pealed with deafening din,
As from the mouth of culverin;
As if aërial hosts on high
Waged strife sublime for victory.
And whizzing balls with musket knell
Like wintry hail descending fell;

And o'er them martial music past,
With rolling drum and clarion blast;
And trampling steeds, with thunder shod,
O'er heaven's rebounding arches trod.
They talked of God's immediate hand
Outstretched above the suffering land;
Of timely rains that often came,
To quench the fiercely conquering flame,
That wrapt their homes in helpless hour—
They spoke, and blest the saving power.
And long, to while the hours away,
They talk of many a former day;
Of native hill and peaceful plain,
Far o'er the wild and severing main;
While some with anxious speech prepare
The future councils of the war.

XIX.

Upon a hillock's tufted breast,
Holding no converse with the rest,
An aged man there sate;

Care seemed enstampt upon his front
As if he had endured the brunt
  Of long and adverse fate.
Scarce sixty winters' snows were spread
Upon his venerable head;
And still within his full gray eye
There was a tameless energy,
That told a heart enured to bear
Each form of wo without despair,
And stands aloof, unchilled by sorrow,
No cheer from earthly hope to borrow.
Religion's promise in his view
Was fixed, and he believed it true;
Star of his soul! in glory beaming,
A light worth all earth's sweetest dreaming!
As many a busy murmur fell
  On his scarce conscious ear,
At times to memory, audible,
They told of vanished scenes, too well
  Remembered, and too dear.
Still at some half-caught sentence rose
The troublous image of his woes;

He heard them speak of distant land,
And memory with obtrusive hand
Would point his vision there;
He heard them tell of tender ties,
And the full tide of agonies
Rushed o'er his soul left sad and lone;
A deep, involuntary groan
The inward conflict told;
It was so strange for him to show,
Such outward sign of secret wo,
That silence followed straight, profound,
As if at supernatural sound;
And every speaker's eye around
Turned on that warrior old.
Oft had they longed in vain to hear
That ancient man, of life austere,
His trials dark relate;
For his stern mien, his sadness mixt
With lines of wo subdued, had fixt
Their interest on his fate:
But sorrow's sacred mystery
Can reverential sympathy
In every heart create;

That long-drawn sigh, that burst unchecked,
Appeared to break the spell respect
Had thrown around his fortunes wrecked,
  Lone misery's robe of state!
And they besought him to disclose,
At large, the story of his woes.

XX.

It seemed that feeling's bursting tide
Had half o'erborne the silent pride,
That barred communion with its pain,
And made the wish to comfort vain.
A struggle passed, intense and brief,
While thus began his tale of grief.
"Dark even in youth the orphan's fate,
But youth is ne'er quite desolate;
Its tears revive with moisture sweet,
The wild flowers springing at its feet;
And round in goodly prospect rise
Green, smooth ascents, and cloudless skies.
For who, when fancy warm and young,
Depicts the future's dazzling scope,

Lists not the charmer's syren tongue,
Owns not the power of suasive hope?
Would that in after years of grief,
I could have felt the sadness brief
That infancy bestows!
Would that my heart by madness wrung,
To hope's sweet comfort could have clung,
Amid severer woes!
But rolling years of varied sorrow,
Have bade me nought from hope to borrow;
Far is her flight, and strong her wing,
And eagle-like her foot will cling,
Above the storm, to cliffs that raise
Their fronts to catch the solar blaze.
Yet lives she not amid the skies,
Like eastern birds of Paradise,
Whose food in fragrant air is given,
Who quaff the balmy dews of heaven:
Deserted on her eyry high,
Her bosom faints, and fails her eye,
And hope herself unfed will die.

Who follows not the torch of hope,
Shall in no future darkness grope;
Who builds not on her promise fair,
Needs fear no earthquake of despair.

XXI.

"I had a brother whom I loved,
The only kindred death had left;
And wo our mutual friendship proved,
Of those who cherished us bereft.
I loved him—and he clung to me,
Though nearly young and weak as he;
For friends were cold; and coldness made
Us seek each other's feeble aid.
And oft together would we mourn
O'er days that never could return;
We wept for those whom memory still
Would to our youthful hearts reveal;
We wandered to their sepulchre,—
For all we loved was resting there:
Where oft till midnight we would stay,
And watch, and weep again, and pray;

Till seemed in our young bosoms shed,
A fellow-feeling with the dead.

XXII.

" We parted, when a venturous band
In quest of wealth, to foreign land,
  The aspiring Edward drew;
'Twas with a deep, foreboding gloom
Beside our parents' sacred tomb,
  We spoke our last adieu.
And tidings rare and far between,
Told where the wanderer's steps had been;
Till silence o'er his fate was spread,
And when long years had come and fled,
I deemed him numbered with the dead.
But now, to blast the realm's repose,
The banner dark of discord rose,
And friends became each other's foes
  In that unnatural war:
My soul was young, untutored then,
In all the evil ways of men;

And liberty's insulted name,
Set all my bosom in a flame,
The glorious strife to share.
The infant's inexperienced sight
Of distance cannot judge aright;
And youthful dreams will still deceive,
And youthful bosoms still believe,
When passion has the sway:
Alas! that time can but disclose
The snares that trap the soul's repose,
In youth's misguided day!
When wisdom learns too late to shun
The snares by which we were undone,—
In age's dim decay.

XXIII.

"Grand, but delusive, is the dream,
When dazzling rays of glory seem,
With light celestial, to illume
The burnished crest, and dancing plume;
When angel tones are heard to fill
The trump's inspiring clamours shrill;

When the mailed host, in stern array,
Rolls onward with resistless sway;
While with one pulse each heart beats high,
One sacred fire in every eye,
And one the unbroken battle cry,
'For conscience and for liberty!'
The cause for which I fought and bled,
Is dear, though all its hopes have fled,—
Fled from our country's ark, to trace
In western wilds a resting place,
Where yet, in solemn groves, the soul
Communes with heaven without control,
And, like the Patriarch in the wood,
Invokes the everlasting God!

XXIV.

"It boots not now with pains to tell
Of all that in that war befell;
How king and state with various chance
Encountered each the other's lance;
How, bleeding fresh from every pore,
Our country weltered in her gore;

While every breeze that swept the sky
Told but of war's wild revelry;
When even the brother had imbrued
His hands amid his brother's blood;—
The parent wept no more his son,
In that disastrous strife undone;
For all was hostile;—all arose
To fill the cup of England's woes.

XXV.

"It was on Naseby's fatal plain
Our host was marshalled once again;
And, on their common soil, for blood
The kindred ranks impatient stood.
While CHARLES and RUPERT on the right
In triumph brief maintained the fight,
I followed CROMWELL's sage command,
Where LANGDALE led his loyal band,
And vainly strove to check the tide
That all his vigilance defied.
Routed and broken as he flew,
More wide the scattering slaughter grew.

I marked a gallant warrior long
At bay restrain the impetuous throng;
Fierce fell the flashes of his blade,
Like lightning on the foeman's head;
And death was dealt in every wound,
Till parted his assailants round;
I marked him, where alone, amain
His courser scoured the encumbered plain:
Filled with the fury of the day,
I followed reckless on his way;
Fainter and faltering in their course,
The blood drops fell from knight and horse;
He turned, as my descending sword
Through the reft mail his bosom gored,
Then sunk, his fleeting vigour gone;—
The staggering steed rushed blindly on;—
O God! as round my victim gazed,
His eye with death's dull amel glazed,
I saw my brother in my foe!
And he his murderer seemed to know—
For pardon lingered in his eye,
As death's drear shadow flitted by;—

His lips essaying seemed to sever,
But quivering vainly, closed for ever!

XXVI.

"No more with martial zeal inspired,
To a lone valley I retired,
To spend what yet remained of years
In penitential thoughts and tears:
But sadness came as horror past,
New objects charmed my soul at last,
And from my wounded core anew
A scion green of promise grew.
I loved—was blest—'tis briefly said—
As swift those blissful moments fled:
The angel partner who had smiled
On my lone path, through deserts wild,
And led to earth's sole Paradise,
Was wrapt to her congenial skies.

XXVII.

"One pledge she left; I could not brook
Longer upon those scenes to look,

Where ghosts of pain or pleasure past
Started, where'er my glance was cast.
I bore my daughter o'er the flood,
Trembling at ocean's wild alarms,
Just blooming into womanhood,
And ripe in all her mother's charms.
Ye know the rest;—an Indian sought
Ere long our newly rising cot:
It seemed the friendship which he bare
The white man's race had led him there,
With strong desire their love to learn,
And Christian usages discern.
He showed what soil would bear the grain,
What best our scanty herds sustain;
For he had learnt to speak our tongue,
And he would listen, fixed and long,
When of sublimer themes I spoke,
Revealed in inspiration's book;
Unfolding thence the wondrous plan
Of all that God had done for man.
By converse oft, and frequent view,
Almost as one of us he grew;

Yet liked I not sometimes to hear
How he would win my Nora's ear,
With legends of his tawny race,
And feats that Nipnet annals grace.

XXVIII.

"In sooth his form was free and bold,
And cast in nature's noblest mould;
His martial head full lightly bore
The many-tinctured plumes he wore;
His glossy locks beneath their band
Were clipt with no unskilful hand;
His polished limbs unseamed with scars,
And wonted stains of Indian wars—
And well the robe we gave became
With graceful fold his goodly frame.
Frank was his speech; but ne'er would rove,
Tutored by cunning, or by love,
To themes for woman's ear unfit:
And Nora listening long would sit,
By words and signs while he expressed
Creation's wonders in the west;

Or told of foughten field; or showed
Through woods and wolds the hunter's road;
How plain, and swamp, and forest through,
They chased the mighty buffalo;
Or winged the unerring arrow, where
High coiling in his leafy lair,
They saw the panther's eyeballs glare.
Of ambush base and torture fell,
Of midnight fire and murderous yell,
Of blood-stained rites and league with hell,
The treacherous spoiler did not tell!
And she would ask to hear again
The feats of wild and martial men;
Or told in turn, what art had done,
In lands beyond the rising sun;
Of those vast hives of human homes;
Proud palaces and glittering domes;
Of loaded quays, and sails that bear
From all the globe their tribute there;
Of armies in their panoply,
And floating bulwarks on the sea.

Yet little marvelled he, at all
The pomp her memory could recall.
But better was she pleased, to tell
Of her own loved and pastoral vale,
Its sheltering hills, and banks of green,
Of childhood's gladsome pranks the scene.
Then rapt, his ear he would incline,
As if some seraph's voice divine
Brought tidings from those opal fields
Which Autumn's sun, descending, gilds.
I should have looked to see as soon
The uncavernned wolf, in frolics boon,
With bounding fawn unfeared agree,
As that between *them* love should be.
But I abhorred such converse vain,
And checked the Pagan's speech profane.
I chided and forbade. Alas!
Too late to save my child it was.
Perchance, too long alone she strayed,
In her young hours, within the shade
Of those blest scenes where life began,
Far from the busy haunts of man.

For sinful phantasy still loves
To people mountains, caves and groves;
By whispering leaves and murmuring rill,
The tempter speaks, when all is still,
And phantoms in the brain will raise,
That haunt the paths of after days.
Weeds o'er the uncultured mind will spread,
As fern from earth's neglected bed.
Perchance, and I believe it true,
Of herb and spell the powers he knew;
Tutored in their foul jugglers' art,
By fiendish craft he won her heart.

XXIX.

"I drove the Pagan forth too late,
For they at stolen hours had met;—
Haply, too sternly to my child
I spoke; her nature was most mild,
Her feelings warm, but never wild.
I trod too rudely on the shoot
Of that young passion's embryo root;

Like the meek chamomile, it grew
Luxuriant from the bruise anew.
An English youth her suitor came;
I hoped to quench the unholy flame
The heathen lit, by sacred vows
Of wedlock with a Christian spouse.
It did but haste her final doom,—
On one sad night she left her home;
She parted, with the tawny chief,
And left me lonely in my grief.
Research was vain, though long pursued,
I sought again my solitude:——
She sowed the winds that madly blew,—
She could but reap the whirlwind too!
'Twas cruel, in the stranger's clime,
Thus from her gray old sire to part,
And barb the only shaft that time
Had yet in store to pierce my heart.
But O, my child! where'er thou art—
Whether beneath the inclement sky,
Thy whitening bones unburied lie;

Or dead alone in damning sin,
Thou sharest the apostate's slough unclean,
This, this the undying source of pain,
We cannot meet in heaven again!
Is it not written—'when thy God
Shall make the nations' realm thine own,
Thou shalt not mingle with their blood,
Nor yield thy daughter to his son.
For from the path her fathers trod,
Her steps to idols will be won;
And swift destruction's fiery doom
The accursëd union shall consume!'"

XXX.

Fitzgerald ceased; and every eye
Paid tribute to his agony:
Even hearts were moved, long hardened made,
By cold, deliberate murder's trade.
On rough-worn features, stern and rude,
The glistening tear unwonted stood;
As on the gnarled oak's scathëd boughs,
The dew-drop of the morning glows.

Scarce had he paused, when through the wood,
Up to the camp, two horsemen rode,
Wayworn, as if with tidings bound;
And quick, their panting coursers round,
The troop impatient thronged, to hear
What news they brought of hope or fear.
Right glad their leader was, to view,
His former comrades, bold and true;
And loud the joyous murmurs broke,
As thus the elder soldier spoke.

XXXI.

"News from the SACHEM! trapt at last,
In his own den we hold him fast,
An Indian from the rebel fled,
Incensed for blood of kindred shed,
From Haup's wild fastnesses last night
Escaped, and beckoning met our sight.
Brought from the adverse bank, he told
Where now the traitor keeps his hold;
And bade us haste, from murderous knife,
If we would save a Christian's life.

On secret enterprise, a band
Had sought, by METACOM's command,
At eventide, the island shore,
Its central forests to explore.
And with them had his friend been sent,
Who told him of their black intent,
Some secret foul, which but those few
Of PHILIP's trusted followers knew.
Brief time for rescue was allowed,
We took what followers chance bestowed;—
Swift was our journey; but 'twas yet,
To intercept the foe too late.
Just on the bank their band we met,
And one, beneath our instant shot,
Was stretched in death upon the spot.
The rest in terror o'er the flood,
Through the dim shades their flight made good.
Clasped by the friendly Indian there,
A Christian woman, young and fair,
Fainted we found; the Indian's art
Recalled the life-pulse to her heart,

The living lustre to her eye,
Which only gazed on vacancy :—
Her child was gone—her cry was vain,
And feverish madness fir'd her brain;
On woven boughs and leaves upborne,
We brought the unconscious dame forlorn.
Through tangled brake and forest screen
Long has our toilsome journey been :—
Waste we no more of idle breath,
But hunt the outlaw to the death!"

XXXII.

Meantime, the oaks' tall columns through,
The expected band appeared in view;
Slow through the glade their steps advance;
Locked in a calm and deathlike trance,
With them the rescued dame was brought,
Free from the agonies of thought.
Near, in an opening of the wood,
A long-forsaken wigwam stood.
Its ruins nought but curious quest
The former haunt of men had guessed;

For woven saplings, germing new,
Thick round the rustic dwelling grew.
The twisted creeper's verdant woof
O'erspread the boughs, and bearskin tough,
And birchen bark, its simple roof;
And wild flowers mid the foliage twine;
The many-coated columbine,
And bittersweet luxuriant sprung,
Robust and statelier vines among.
Now from that pyramid of green,
A curling smoke was rising seen,
Mid sycamore's o'erarching screen.
A transient shelter it became,
To a poor settler and his dame ;—
Though comfortless such dwelling be,
'Twas yet the home of liberty.—
Straightway the two Mohegans there
The litter with its burden bare.
O'er the fair form, in pitying mood,
The lowly cabin's inmates stood;
They bathed her brow, and raised her head,
Until again her stupor fled :

The circling white of her blue eye
Was stained with redly gushing die;
Streaks which the storm of anguish past,
Across its liquid heaven had cast
Now those bright orbs, with wandering roll,
Betrayed the twilight of the soul;
And now a shriek, on every ear,
Fell, like lost wretch's cry of fear,
When toppling from the dizzy steep,
He sinks into the roaring deep!
FITZGERALD heard that frenzied cry—
It struck on his bosom suddenly,
Like a chord's sad sound, when bursting near,
From a harp whose music was most dear.

XXXIII.

He rushed to the hut;—with a start he met
The child he loved too fondly yet;
Up springing wildly at the sight,
Her madness yields to nature's might.
At first the father would have prest
The hapless wanderer to his breast;

But sterner thoughts repulsive rose,
Of all her guilt and all his woes:
While a drear conflict was begun,
And nature now, now anger won,
Pale NORA hid her face to shun
The glance she dared no longer meet:—
Prostrate and trembling at his feet,
She only clasped his knees and wept,
While round her auburn tresses swept:—
She only sighed, in murmurs low,
"O do not curse me!" "Curse thee! no;
Tho' down the vale of years alone,
I bear my cross with tottering frame,
And pangs than death more dread have known,
Pangs from a daughter's hand that came—
I would not call the eternal wrath,
To burst o'er thy misguided path!
Tho' hopeless of forgiveness there,
I can but plead with earnest prayer,
  Against its heavier curse:
Oh! I had borne to see thy bloom
Of youth, slow withering o'er its tomb—
  Had borne to see thy hearse,

Hung with the stainless virgin wreath,
That told thy purity in death.
But thus—from heathen's couch defiled,
Polluted outcast of the wild—
I cannot brook to see my child!"
"Then, then, I am indeed undone,
And light or hope on earth is none!
Here let me die!" "No! sinful one!
Live! rising from the gloomier grave
Of guilt, no more the tempter's slave.
Live! let thy days in tears be spent,
In mental penance deep repent;
Thou art not fit to die!" he said,
And raised the mourner from the ground,
And all his gathered sternness fled,
When in his arms his child he found.
Their tears together blending flow—
Her crime forgiven, almost forgot,
Till severing from her pressure slow,
Calmer he left the lonely cot.
"Nora, farewell! if heaven should spare
Thy sire, his home thou still shalt share;

But if, in this uncertain strife,
An Indian ball destroy my life,
Christians, I know, my child will save;
And, when I moulder in the grave,
Remember—that thy sire forgave."
He left her, but his parting word
His shuddering daughter had not heard;
On adverse sides—her only thought—
Her father and her husband fought.

XXXIV.

Counsel meantime the soldiers hold—
The Indian there his injury told;
He said Ahauton was his name,
And of Mohegan line he came;
Told how the death of Agamoun
A brother's vengeance must atone;
And how to dust by sorrow borne,
By pain, defeat, and famine worn,
The wily Sachem could not hope
Much longer with his foes to cope.

Tho' fiercely yet of war he spoke,
Yet his stout heart was almost broke,
When last were slain, round Taunton's wave,
His counsellors and his warriors brave.
Left now of all his tribe alone,
The Wampanoags' glory gone—
His every friend and kinsman dead,
Soon he must yield his forfeit head.

XXXV.

Their eager conference o'er at last,
The mandate for the march was past.
Swiftly the scanty files withdrew,
As shrill the warning bugle blew;
Their arms thro' thickets glittering bright,
Before the sun's retiring light,
Who, waning from his central throne,
Thro' clouds and forests lurid shone.
The rising wind that shook the trees,
Or curled the waving of the seas;
The shrieking birds that sped along,
Or plunged the rising waves among,

Proclaimed, by signs distinct and clear,
The bursting of a storm was near.
As past the eager troop away,
FITZGERALD made a brief delay,
With the Mohegan chief, before
He joined their march along the shore.
They spoke in low and whispered tone,
But, when their earnest speech was done,
"Lead thou my steps," the old man cried,
"To their foul haunts be thou my guide.
Heaven bids me mar the rites defiled,
And seek and save my daughter's child."

YAMOYDEN.

CANTO IV.

YAMOYDEN.

CANTO FOURTH.

As if to battle, o'er the midnight heaven
The clouds are hurrying forth: now veiled on high,
Now sallying out, the moon and stars are driven,
As wandering doubtful; in the shifting sky,
Mid mazes strange the Dancers seem to fly;
Wildly the unwearied hunters drive the Bear:
Through the deep groves is heard a Spirit's cry;
And hark! what strain unearthly echoes there,
Borne fitful from afar, along the troubled air.

TO THE MANITTO OF DREAMS.

I.

1.

"SPIRIT! THOU SPIRIT of subtlest air,
Whose power is upon the brain,
When wondrous shapes, and dread, and fair,

As the film from the eyes
At thy bidding flies,
To sight and sense are plain!

2.

"Thy whisper creeps where leaves are stirred;
Thou sighest in woodland gale;
Where waters are gushing thy voice is heard;
And when stars are bright,
At still midnight,
Thy symphonies prevail!

3.

"Where the forest ocean, in quick commotion,
Is waving to and fro,
Thy form is seen, in the masses green,
Dimly to come and go.
From thy covert peeping, where thou layest sleeping,
Beside the brawling brook,
Thou art seen to wake, and thy flight to take
Fleet from thy lonely nook.

4.

Where the moonbeam has kist
The sparkling tide,
In thy mantle of mist
Thou art seen to glide.
Far o'er the blue waters
Melting away,
On the distant billow,
As on a pillow,
Thy form to lay.

5.

Where the small clouds of even
Are wreathing in heaven
Their garland of roses,
O'er the purple and gold,
Whose hangings enfold
The hall that encloses
The couch of the sun,
Whose empire is done,—
There thou art smiling,
For thy sway is begun;
Thy shadowy sway,

The senses beguiling,
When the light fades away,
And thy vapour of mystery o'er nature ascending,
The heaven and the earth,
The things that have birth,
And the embryos that float in the future is blending.

II.

1.

"From the land, on whose shores the billows break
The sounding waves of the mighty lake;
From the land where boundless meadows be,
Where the buffalo ranges wild and free;
With silvery coat in his little isle,
Where the beaver plies his ceaseless toil;
The land where pigmy forms abide,
Thou leadest thy train at the even tide;
And the wings of the wind are left behind,
So swift through the pathless air they glide.

2.

Then to the chief who has fasted long,
When the chains of his slumber are heavy and strong,

SPIRIT! thou comest; he lies as dead,
His weary lids are with heaviness weighed;
But his soul is abroad on the hurricane's pinion,
Where foes are met in the rush of fight,
In the shadowy world of thy dominion
Conquering and slaying, till morning light!

3.

Then shall the hunter who waits for thee,
The land of the game rejoicing see;
Through the leafless wood,
O'er the frozen flood,
And the trackless snows
His spirit goes,
Along the sheeted plain,
Where the hermit bear, in his sullen lair,
Keeps his long fast, till the winter hath past,
And the boughs have budded again.
SPIRIT OF DREAMS! all thy visions are true,
Who the shadow hath seen, he the substance shall
view!

III.

1.

"Thine the riddle, strange and dark,
Woven in the dreamy brain:—
Thine to yield the power to mark
Wandering by, the dusky train;
Warrior ghosts for vengeance crying,
Scalped on the lost battle's plain,
Or who died their foes defying,
Slow by lingering tortures slain.

2.

Thou the war-chief hovering near,
Breathest language on his ear;
When his winged words depart,
Swift as arrows to the heart;
When his eye the lightning leaves;
When each valiant bosom heaves;
Through the veins when hot and glowing
Rage like liquid fire is flowing;
Round and round the war pole whirling,
Furious when the dancers grow;

When the maces swift are hurling
Promised vengeance on the foe;
Thine assurance, SPIRIT true!
Glorious victory gives to view!

3.

When of thought and strength despoiled,
Lies the brave man like a child;
When discoloured visions fly,
Painful, o'er his glazing eye,
And wishes wild through his darkness rove,
Like flitting wings through the tangled grove,—
Thine is the wish; the vision thine,
And thy visits, SPIRIT! are all divine!

4.

When the dizzy senses spin,
And the brain is madly reeling,
Like the Pów-wah, when first within
The present spirit feeling;
When rays are flashing athwart the gloom,
Like the dancing lights of the northern heaven,
When voices strange of tumult come
On the ear, like the roar of battle driven,—

The Initiate then shall thy wonders see,
And thy priest, O Spirit! is full of thee!

IV.

"Spirit of dreams! away! away!
It is thine hour of solemn sway;
And thou art holy; and our rite
Forbids thy presence here to-night.
Go light on lids that wake to pain;
Triumphant visions yield again!
If near the Christian's cot thou roam,
Tell him the fire has wrapt his home:
Where the mother lies in peaceful rest,
Her infant slumbering on her breast,
Tell her the red man hath seized its feet,
And against a tree its brains doth beat:
Fly to the bride who sleeps alone,
Her husband forth for battle gone;
Tell her, at morn,—and tell her true,—
His head on the bough her eyes shall view;
While his limbs shall be the raven's prey:—
Spirit of dreams! away! away!"

V.

So sung the Initiates, o'er their rite
While hung the gloom of circling night.
Nor yet the unholy chant must rise,
Nor blaze the fire of sacrifice,
Until behind yon groves afar,
The Bear hath dipt his westering car;
And shrouded night, with central sway,
Veiled deeds unfit to meet the day.
Then rose the Prophet, on whose eye
Past generations had gone by:
He saw them fall, as some vast oak,
By storms unriven, by bolts unbroke,
Sees all the forest by its side
In countless autumns shed its pride;
Marks, gathering still, as years roll on,
Winter's sere harvest round it strown;—
Yet his gigantic form ascends,
Nor to the howling voice of time,
One sturdy, veteran sinew bends,
Erect in native grace sublime.

The scattered relics of the lock,
Which oft had waved o'er battle shock,
In long and silvery lines were spread,
Like the white honours o'er the head
  Of ancient mountain ash ;—
His large eyes brightly, coldly shone,
As if their mortal light was gone
  With clear, unearthly flash ;
With strong arms forth outstretched he sprung ;
Loose o'er his frame the bearskin hung ;
Through every limb quick tremors ran,
As, rapt with fate, that aged man
His lore oracular began.

VI.

The Prophecy.

" O heard ye around the sad moan of the gale,
As it sighed o'er the mountain, and shrieked in the
    vale ?
'Tis the voice of the Spirit prophetic, who past ;
His mantle of darkness around him is cast ;

Wild flutters his robe, and the light of his plume
Faint glimmers along through the mist and the
gloom ;
Where the moonbeam is hidden, the shadow hath
gone,
It has flitted in darkness, that morrow has none ;
But my ear drank the sound, and I feel in my breast,
What the voice of the Spirit prophetic imprest.
O saw ye that gleaming unearthly of light ?
Behold where it winds o'er the moor from our
sight !—
'Tis the soul of a warrior who sleeps with the slain;—
How long shall the slaughtered thus wander in vain?
It has past ; through the gloom of the forest it flies,—
But I feel in my bosom its murmurs arise.

VII.

" Say, what are the races of perishing men ?
They darken earth's surface, and vanish agen ;
As the shade o'er the lake's gleaming bosom that
flies,
With the stir of their wings where the wildfowl arise,

That has past,—and the sunbeam plays bright as
before,—
So speed generations, remembered no more;
Since earth from the deep, at the voice of the spirit,
Rose green from the waters, with all that inherit
Its nature, its changes. The oaks that had stood
For ages, lie crumbling at length in the wood.
Where now are the race in their might who came
forth,
To destroy and to waste, from the plains of the north?
As the deer through the brake, mid the forests they
sped,
The tall trees crashed round them; earth groaned
with their tread;
He perished, the Mammoth,—in power and in pride,
And defying the wrath of Yohewah he died!
And say, what is man, that his race should endure,
Alone through the changes of nature secure?
Where now are the giants, the soil who possest,
When our fathers came down, from the land of the
west?

The grass o'er their mounds and their fortresses
waves,
And choaked amid weeds are the stones on their
graves;
The hunter yet lingers in wonder, where keeps
The rock on the mountains the track of their steps;
Nor other memorial remains there, nor trace,
Of the proud ALLEGEWI's invincible race.

VIII.

"As their nation was slain by the hands of our sires,
Our race, in its turn, from our country expires!
Lo! even like some tree, where a Spirit before
Had dwelt, when rich garlands and offerings it bore,
But now, half uptorn from its bed in the sands,
By the wild waves encroaching, that desolate stands,
Despoiled of the pride of its foliage and fruit,
While its branches are naked, and bare is its root;—
And each surge that returns still is wearing its bed,
Till it falls, and the ocean rolls on overhead;—
Nor a wreck on the shore, nor a track on the flood,
Tells aught of the trunk that so gloriously stood,—

Even so shall our nations, the children of earth,
Return to that bosom that yielded them birth.
Ye tribes of the Eagle, the Panther, and Wolf!
Deep sunk lie your names in a fathomless gulf!
Your war-whoop's last echo has died on the shore;
The smoke of your wigwams is curling no more.
Mourn, land of my fathers! thy children are dead;
Like the mists in the sunbeam, thy warriors have
fled!

IX.

"But a Spirit there is, who his presence enshrouds,
Enthroned on our hills in his mantle of clouds.
He speaks in the whirlwind; the river outpours
Its tribute to him, where the cataract roars.
His breath is the air we inhale; and his reign
Shall endure till the waters have triumphed again;
Till the earth's deep foundation convulsions shall
heave,
And the bosom of darkness its fabric receive!
'Tis the spirit of freedom! and ne'er shall our
grave
Be trod by the recreant, or spurned by the slave!

And lo! as the vision of years rolls away,
When our tribes shall have past, and the victor hath
sway,
That spirit I mark o'er the war-cloud presiding;
The storm that rolls upward sublime he is guiding;
It is bursting in terror; and choked is the path
Of peace, by the ruins it whelms in its wrath.
The rivers run blood; and the war-caldron boils,
By the flame of their cities, the blaze of their spoils.
Bend, bend from your clouds, and rejoice in the
sight,
Ye ghosts of the red men! for freedom they fight!

X.

"Dim visions! why crowd ye so fast o'er my eyes,
In the twilight of days that are yet to arise?
Undefined are the shapes and the masses that
sweep,
Like the hurricane clouds, o'er the face of the
deep;
They rise like the waves on the surf-beaten shore,
But recede ere they form, to be gazed on no more.

Like the swarms of the doves o'er the meads that
descend,
From the north's frozen regions their course when
they bend,
So quick o'er our plains is the multitude's motion;
Still the white sails gleam thick o'er the bosom of
ocean;
As the foam of their furrows is lost in the sea,
So *they* melt in one nation, united and free!

XI.

"Mourn, land of my fathers! the red men have past,
Like the strown leaves of Autumn, dispersed by the
blast!
Mourn, land of the victor! a curse shall remain,
Till appeased in their clime are the ghosts of the
slain!
Like the plants that by pure hands of virgins alone
Must be plucked, or their charm and their virtue is
gone,
So the fair fruits of freedom, souls only can taste,
That are stained by no crime, by no passion debased.

His nest where the foul bird of avarice hath made,
The songsters in terror take wing from the shade;
And man, if unclean in his bosom the fire,
No holier spirits descend to inspire.
Mourn, land of the victor! our curse shall remain,
Till appeased for their wrongs be the souls of the slain!"

XII.

He ceased, and sunk exhausted down,
Strength, fire, and inspiration gone.
The fear-struck savages in vain
Await the unfolding voice again.
A panic terror o'er them ran,
As now their impious task began.
Their pyre was reared on stones that fell,
What time, their fathers' legends tell,
The avenging Spirit's fiery breath
Had poured the withering storm of death
Along that field of blood and shame;
Where now, for ages past the same,
There grew no blade of cheerful green;
But sere and shivering trees were seen,

Blasted, and white with age, to stand,
Like spectres on the accursëd land.
Therewith, meet sacrifice of guilt,
Broad and high-reared, their pile was built.
And now their torch unclean they bear;
Long had they fed its light with care,
Stolen, where polluted walls were razed,
And purifying flames had blazed.

XIII.

Swift o'er the structure climbs the fire;
In serpent course its streams aspire;
Entwined about their crackling prey,
Aloft they shoot with spiral way;
Wreathing and flashing fiercely round,
Their glittering net was mingling wound
O'er all the pile; but soon they blended;
One mighty volume then ascended,—
A column dense of mounting flame:—
Blacker the shrouded heaven became,
And like substantial darkness frowned
O'er the red atmosphere; around

The sands gave back the unnatural glare;
Lifting their ghostly arms in air,
Were seen those trunks all bleak and bare;
At distance rose the giant pine,
Kindling, as if by power divine,
Of fire a living tree;
While, where the circling forests sweep,
Each varying hue, or bright or deep,
Shone, as if raised o'er nature's sleep,
By magic's witchery.

XIV.

He who had marked the Pów-wahs then,
As round the pyre their rites begun,
Had deemed it no vision of mortal men,
But of souls tormented in endless pain,
Who for penance awhile to earth again
Had come to the scene where their crime was done.
No other robe by the band was worn,
Save their girdles rude from the otter torn;
Below, besmeared with sable stain,
Above, blood-red was the fiendish train,

Save a circle pale around each eye,
That shone in the glare with a fiery die;
While a bird with coal-black wings outspread
Was the omen of ill on every head.
And wild their serpent tresses wound,
Unkempt and unconfined around;
For unpurified, since their vows, had been
Those ministers of rites unclean.
And one there was, round whose limbs was coiled
The scaly coat of a snake despoiled;
The jaws by his cheek that open stood,
Seemed clogged and dripping yet with blood.
With the rattling chichicoe he led,
Or swift, or slow, their measured tread;
And wildly flapped, the band among,
The dusky tuft from his staff that hung;
Where the hawk's, the crow's and raven's feather,
With the bat's foul wings were woven together.

XV.

Close by a couch, with mats o'erspread,
As if a pall that wrapt the dead,

Sat crouching one, who might beseem
The goblin crew of a monstrous dream;
For never did earthly creature wear
A shape like that recumbent there.
No hideous brute that starving sought
Some cavern's grisly womb, to rot,
Nor squalid want, in death forlorn,
Hath e'er such haggard semblance borne.
A woman once;—but now a thing
That seemed perverse to life to cling,
To rob the worm of tribute due;—
Her limbs no vesture covering,
No season's change, nor shame she knew.
Burnt on her withered breast she bore
Strange characters of savage lore;
And gathering up her bony frame,
As fiercely raged the mounting flame,
Not one proportion equal told
Of aught designed in nature's mould.
Her yellow eyeballs, bright with hate,
Rolled in their sunken sockets yet,

With sickly glare, as of charnel lamps
That glimmer from sepulchral damps.

XVI.

And now began the Initiates' dance;
Slow they recede, and slow advance;
Hand locked in hand, with footsteps slow,
About the ascending flame they go.
At first, in solemn movement led,
A chant low muttered they obeyed;
But shrill and quick as the measure grew,
Whirling about the pyre they flew,
In a dizzy ring, till their senses reeled,
And the heavens above them madly wheeled,
And the earth spun round, with its surface burning,
Like a thousand fiery circles turning.
Louder and wilder as waxed the tone,
They sever, in uncouth postures thrown;
They sink, they tower, and crouch, and creep,
High mid the darting fire they leap,
And with fearful prank and hellish game,
Disport, as buoyant on the flame.

Now terror seemed to freeze each heart,
As tremulous in every part,
With outstretched arms and wandering eyes,
They brave aërial enemies,
And combat with an unseen foe;
He seems to strike above, below;—
And fiercer grew the imagined fight,
Till every limb, convulsed and tight,
Showed the muscle strained, and swollen vein,
As of madman writhing in mortal pain.
With fury blind, they rolled around,
Impervious to the scorching ground,
And even within the glowing verge
Unconscious and unheeding urge.
The measure changes; ere its close,
Staggering the rout possessed arose;
  Then pealed the loud *hah-hah!*
Harsh, dissonant, in anguish heaved,
As if the soul, to be relieved,
  In sound took wing afar.
Like laughter of exulting fiends,
The startling chorus wild ascends;

While the shrill whoop,—that had seemed to die
With the last breath of agony,
Then rose with its horrid shriek and long,—
Closed that disturbed, discordant song.
Then in the silence, you had thought
The dæmon coming whom they sought,
And from the sullen chichicoe,
Had heard his boding answer flow.

XVII.

Song of the Pow-Wahs.

"Beyond the hills the Spirit sleeps,
His watch the Power of evil keeps;
The Spirit of fire has sought his bed,
The Sun, the hateful Sun is dead.
Profound and clear is the sounding wave,
In the chambers of the Wakon-cave;
Darkness its ancient portal keeps;
And there the Spirit sleeps,—he sleeps.

XVIII.

"Come round on raven pinions now,
Spirits of ill, to you we bow!

Whether ye sit on the topmost cliff,
  While the storm around is sweeping,
Mid the thunder shock, from rock to rock
  To view the lightning leaping;
As ye guide the bolt, where towers afar
  The knotted pine to heaven,
And where it falls, your serpent scar
  On the blasted trunk is graven :—
Whether your awful voices pour
Their tones in gales that nightly roar ;—
Whether ye dwell beneath the lake ;
In whose depths eternal thunders wake,—
Gigantic guard the glittering ore,
That lights Maurepas' haunted shore,—
On Manataulin's lonely isle,
The wanderer of the wave beguile,—
Or love the shore where the serpent-hiss,
And angry rattle never cease,—
Come round on raven pinions now !
SPIRITS OF EVIL ! to you we bow.

XIX.

" Come ye hither, who o'er the thatch
Of the coward murderer hold your watch;
Moping and chattering round who fly
Where the putrid members reeking lie,
Piece-meal dropping, as they decay,
O'er the shuddering recreant day by day;
Till he loathes the food that is whelmed amid
The relics, by foul corruption hid;
And the crawling worms about him bred
Mistake the living for the dead!

XX.

" Come ye who give power
To the curse that is said,
And a charm that shall wither
To the drops that are shed,
On the cheek of the maiden,
Who never shall hear
The kind name of Mother
Saluting her ear;

But sad as the turtle
On the bare branch reclining,
She shall sit in the desert,
Consuming and pining;
With a grief that is silent,
Her beauty shall fade,
Like a flower nipt untimely,
On its stem that is dead.

XXI.

" Come ye who as hawks hover o'er
The spot where the war club is lying,
Defiled with the stain of their gore,
The foemen to battle defying;
On your dusky wings wheeling above,
Who for vengeance and slaughter come crying;
For the scent of the carnage ye love,
The groans of the wounded and dying.

XXII.

" Come ye, who at the sick man's bed,
Watch beside his burning head;

When the vaunting juggler tries in vain
Charm and fast to sooth his pain,
And his fever-balm and herbs applies,
Your death watch ye sound till your victim dies.

XXIII.

" And ye who delight
The soul to affright,
When naked and lonely,
Her dwelling forsaken,
To the country of spirits
Her journey is taken;
When the wings of a dove
She has borrowed to fly,
Ye swoop from above,
And around her ye cry;
She wanders and lingers
In terror and pain,
While the souls of her kindred
Expect her in vain.

XXIV.

" By all the hopes that we forswear;
By the potent rite we here prepare;
By every shriek whose echo falls
Around the Spirits' golden walls;
By our eternal league made good;
By all our wrongs and all our blood;
By the red battle-axe uptorn;
By the deep vengeance we have sworn;
By the uprooted trunk of peace,
And by the wrath that shall not cease,
Where'er ye be, above, below,
Spirits of ill! we call ye now!

XXV.

" Not beneath the mantle blue
Spread below Yohewah's feet;
Not through realms of azure hue
Incense breathing to his seat;
Not with fire, by living light
Kindled from the orb of glory;

Not with words of sacred might,
Taught us in our fathers' story;
Not with odours, fruit or flower,
Thee we summon, dreadful Power!
Power of darkness! Power of ill!
Present in the heart and will,
Plotting, despite of faith and trust,
Treason, avarice, murder, lust!
From caverns deep of gloom and blood,
Attend our call, O serpent God!
Thee we summon by our rite,
Hobamóqui! Power of night!

XVI.

"Behold the sacrifice!
A harmless infant dies,
To whet thine anger's edge;
A Christian woman's pledge,
Begot by Indian sire,
Ascends thy midnight pyre.
For thy friendship, for our wrongs,
To thee the child belongs."

XVII.

Did the fiend hear and answer make?
Above them loud the thunders break;
The livid lightning's pallid hue
Their dusky canopy shone through;
Then tenfold blackness gathering far
Presaged the elemental war.
While yet in air the descant rung,
Upward the listening priestess sprung,
By instant impulse; as if yet
The spirit of her youth survived,
As if from that lethargic state,
Quickened by power vouchsafed, she lived.
She tore the sable mats away,
And there YAMOYDEN's infant lay,
By potent opiates lulled to keep
The silence of the dreamless sleep,
O'er which that night should sink;
Swathed in the sacrificial vest,
Its bier the unconscious victim prest.
The hag's long, shrivelled fingers clasp
The babe in their infernal grasp,

While o'er the fiery brink,
Rapidly, giddily she hurls
The child, as her withered form she whirls;
And chants, with accents hoarse and strong,
The last, the dedicating song.

XXVIII.

Song of the Priestess.

"The black clouds are moving
Athwart the dull moon,
The hawks high are roving,
The strife shall be soon.
Then burst thou deep thunder!
Pour down all ye floods!
Ye flames rive in sunder
The pride of the woods!
But O thou! who guidest
The flood and the fire,
In lightning who ridest,
Directing its ire;—
If darker to-morrow
The wrath of the strife,

Be the white man's the sorrow,
And thine be his life!
The elk-skin about him,
The crow-skin above,
To thee we devote him,
The pledge of mixed love.
For ever and ever
The slaves of thy will,
Let ours be thy favour,
O SPIRIT OF ILL!"

XXIX.

She had not ceased, when on the blast
A warning shriek of horror past;
Emerging from the woodland gloom,
They saw a form unearthly come.
White were its locks, its robes of white,
And gleaming through their lurid light,
Swift it advanced. The Pów-wahs stood,
Palsied amid their rites of blood;
E'en the stern PROPHET feared to trace
The awful features of that face,

And shrunk, as if toward their flame
YOHEWAH's angry presence came.

XXX.

He grasped the witch by her skinny arm,
Her powerless frame confessed the charm;
Before his bright, indignant glance,
Her eyes were fixed in terror's trance.
"Away," the stranger cried, "away!
Votaries of Moloch! yield your prey!
Have ye not heard the wrath on high
Speak o'er your foul iniquity?
Know ye not, for such worship fell,
Deep yawns the eternal gulf of hell?"
Then, bursting from his dream of fear,
To front the intruder rushed the SEER,—
When straight, o'er all the vaulted heaven,
Kindled and streamed the glittering levin;
Pale and discoloured shone below
The embers in that general glow,
As blind amid the blaze they reel,
Rattled and crashed the deafening peal;

And with its voice so long and loud,
Fell the burst torrent from the cloud;
It dashed impetuous o'er the pile;
The hissing waters rave and boil;
The smothered fires a moment soar,
Spread their swarth glare the forest o'er,
Then sink beneath their whelming pall,
And total darkness covers all.

XXXI.

O many a shriek of horror fell,
Amid that darkness terrible,
Unlit, save by the lightning's flash,
And echoing with the tempest crash
Those stifled screams of fear;
They deem in every bursting peal
The avenging Spirits' rage they feel,
And crouching, shuddering hear.
While ever and anon ascended
The dying PRIESTESS' maddened cry,—
With muttering curses fearful blended
It rose convulsed on high.

And when their palsying dread was gone,
And a dim brand recovered shone,
And when they traced by that sad light
The scene of their unfinished rite,
And many a look uncertain cast,
The STRANGER and the CHILD had past.

YAMOYDEN.

CANTO V.

YAMOYDEN.

CANTO FIFTH.

'Tis night; the loud wind through the forest wakes,
With sound like ocean's roaring, wild and deep,
And in yon gloomy pines strange music makes,
Like symphonies unearthly, heard in sleep;
The sobbing waters dash their waves and weep;
Where moans the blast its dreary path along,
The bending firs a mournful cadence keep;
And mountain rocks re-echo to the song,
As fitful raves the storm, the hills and woods among.

I.

What wanderer finds his way to-night,
Amid the forest's depth of gloom,
Where gleams no ray of lingering light
The horrid darkness to illume;
Save where the lightning's dazzling stream
Descends with momentary gleam?

O'er his high form and plumëd head,
The thick and heavy drops were shed;
While round there fell upon his ear
Many a sound for doubt and fear;
The wolf's fierce howl at distance heard;
The screaming of each startled bird;
At times the falling forest's crash,
Scattered by the rending flash,
Mingled with the tempest's wrath,
Around that lonely wanderer's path.

II.

Across the strait, whose heaving wave,
When rising gusts impetuous rave,
And gales are sweeping on their way,
From isle to isle and bay to bay,
Wakes, lashed to foam, with fury strong,
To join the chorus of their song,
Yamoyden sought the island shore,
Despite of all the billowy roar;
And onward through the tangled path,
Sped, heedless of the tempest's wrath.

Swifter his cautious footsteps grew,
When near, his NORA's bower he krew.
A gleam prolonged of lightning showed
The limit of his darksome road;
Pale, but distinct, its lustre played,
Lambent along the narrow glade :—
Where yon old elm its arm extends,
That slowly o'er his pathway bends,
With solemn gesture, as if meant
To warn the wanderer of intent
  Unknown, or danger near,—
Does fancy's mimic dread portray
Amid the boughs a spectre gray,
Or is it the boding vision seen,
Where murder's secret work has been,
  Oft by the Indian seer?
Ha! points it to the cottage now?
Fled from his heart the rising glow,
And gushing stood upon his brow,
  The damps of awful fear.

III.

That moment ceased the tempest's sound,
As if its spirits hovering round,
Listening the wanderer's tread,
Awhile withheld their deafening yell;
And a hushed pause about him fell,
The silence of the dead.
The thunder was no longer heard;
No breath the dripping forest stirred:
There only murmured far away,
Solemnly the moaning bay;—
The faint sigh of the sinking breeze
Rustled amid the farthest trees;
The rain drops from the loaded spray
With sullen plash around him sunk;—
Then paused the wanderer on his way;
Bowed to foreboding terror's sway
His soul within him shrunk.

IV.

The cottage of his hope is near;
But came no sound upon his ear;

No trembling taper twinkled dim,
To tell of vigils kept for him.
Perchance she sleeps; he onward past;
The humble roof is gained at last;
He paused awhile to listen there,—
'Twas still and solemn as despair;
He called,—none answered to his call,—
He entered,—it was darkness all.
It struck to his heart with a deadly chill,
That horrid darkness, deep and still;
Stunned was his brain, as with a blow;
And still he seemed not yet to know
The fearful certainty of wo.

V.

As one not heeding why or where,
He staggered back, in the chilly air.
Again the tempest's spirits spoke,
Again the deep-voiced thunder woke,
In lengthening volleys peal on peal,
Whereat earth's fabric seemed to reel;

While, as from caldrons vast, of flame,
Down the o'erwhelming deluge came.
Died on his ear, unheard, the roar;
He had not recked although before
His step the earth had yawned;
Though all the imagined shapes and forms
That drive to battle blackening storms,
In stern array his path had crost;—
In grief's thick darkness he was lost,
On which no daybeam dawned.

VI.

"There is no hope," he murmured, "none!
I journey homeless and alone.
The forest eagle's secret nest
Has seen, at last, the spoiler's quest.
O'er life's remaining wastes of wo,
Alone, and desperate, forth I go.
Fool that I was, who vainly thought,
When ruin's work was round me wrought,
Amid a people's funeral cry,
Still to secure that only tie,—

That flower which, with too venturous hand,
From danger's topmost steep I bore;
And fostered, in a desert land,
Amid the gaunt wolves' raving band,
Amid the whirlwind's ceaseless roar.
And yet it grew, mid doubt and fear,
And desolation round, more dear;
And still was every care it brought,
Affection's agony of thought,
That tore the heart, and racked the brain,
Blest in the sacred source of pain.
Like some lone bird, whose pinions hover,
Flapping and tired, as on she hies,
The lake's far gleaming surface over,
Who now a seeming reed espies,
Where, mid the waters, she may rest
Her drooping head and weary breast,
Then trusting to that guileful stay,
Becomes the lurking monster's prey,
Her heart by fangs relentless torn
Even from that dearly welcomed bourne;

So I, a wanderer lone, had fain
On love's confiding bosom lain;
To find, where all the rest had past,
Thence came the deadliest wound at last,
And that fond shelter vain.
Vain! shall I seek her father's hall,
Where she must pine in dreary thrall,
Reproach her portion sad in life,
Who dared to be the Indian's wife?
Shall I forsake our brethren left,
Of power, of kin, of home bereft;
Even the vile fox's part essay,
And point the ruffians to their prey?
Idle the dastard treachery were,
They would not yield her to my prayer.
O Nora! if one beam of hope
Could through unfathomed darkness grope,
For thee, thy child, thy God, I dare
All but a traitor's name to bear;
All the proud heart must bend to brook,
Soothed by thy one atoning look.

For thee, for them, I once have borne
Thy father's wrath, thy kinsmen's scorn,
Their pledge of peace they tear away,
And vengeance hath its debt to pay.

VII.

" Roar on ye winds! your voice must be
Sweet as the bridal chant to me.
Widowed in love, with hate I wed,
Espoused within her gory bed.
The storm of heaven will soon be past,
And all be bright and calm at last;
But man in cruelty and wrong
The tempest's fury will prolong,
And pause not in his fell career
Save o'er my brethren's general bier.
Then come my foes! your work is done!
I cannot weep, I will not groan.
Thy fathers winced not at the stake,
Nor gave revenge, with torture rife,
One drop its burning thirst to slake,
To the last ebbing drop of life.

My heart is cold and desolate;—
I shall not struggle long with fate.
Had I a mortal foe, and were
His form to rise upon me here,
There is no power within my soul,
My arm or weapon to control;—
Sunken and cold! but it will rise,
With my lost tribe's last battle cries;
And death will come, like the last play
Of lightning on a stormy day!"

VIII.

So mused the chieftain as he strode
Backward upon his cheerless road.
The shore is nigh; the storm again
Had hushed its mad and clamorous strain;
There was a roar along the surge,
Which howling winds had ceased to urge;
The dark gray clouds above were spread,
In softening aspect, overhead;
The lightning faint at distance played,
  And low the thunders die.

Most melancholy was the sound
Of murmuring winds and waters round;
And sadly showed the tempest's path,
Where yet the signals of its wrath
  Were hung in grandeur high.
Dark flowed the rapid waves beneath,
Save where the levin's lessening wreath
  Yet trembled in the sky;
Painted the feathery surge upon,
Its flash in dying glory shone,
  And vanished fitfully.
It was an hour for one to mourn,
In life, in love, in hope forlorn;
When all obove, and all below,
Pour their deep thrill on heart of wo,
  Lone sorrow's luxury;—
As oft there gleams a transient glow,
Above the headlong torrent's flow,
  To sooth and cheer the eye;
With its half lost and filmy ray,
Lingering upon the restless spray,
  As fleets the current by.

IX.

Once more his bark is on the wave,
To join the desperate and the brave;
On through the heaving bay it flew,
As his strong arm behind him threw
The crested wave; unheedful still,
While strength exerts its wonted skill,
He only felt, his heart around,
A girth that all its pulses bound;
And all of memory, fear or hope,
Was wound within its anguished scope;
As when the fated victim feels
The Carcajou about him dart;
And staggering thro' the forest reels,
While still the foe insidious steals
His mortal pressure round the heart,—
Until the wound his mercy deals,
That lets the struggling soul depart.

X.

Meantime within his trusted hold
The dauntless outlaw lay;

In scapeless peril proud and bold,
  As in his victor day.
The bear mid northern winter's gloom,
In some old oak's sequestered womb,
Lethargic lives, nor tastes of food,
Till from his cheerless solitude,
The exulting voice of balmy spring,
The sullen hermit forth shall bring;
But can the soul, that slumbers never,
Live on, when hope has fled for ever;—
When homage, royalty and power
Have past, the pageant of an hour;—
Live on, through exile, want and chains,
When neither friend nor slave remains;—
Live on, the mark and theme of hate,
To bide the smile of frowning fate,—
The single chance,—not yet to fall,
As vulgar souls resign their breath;—
And bear, with gloomy patience, all,
One trophy to erect in death;
One stab, with dying hand, to give,
And know *one* foeman shall not live?

XI.

Thou, of the ocean rock! what eye
  Thy secret mind shall scan?
No conqueror now, no monarch high;
  A lone, a captive man!
Thine was the chance, in regal sway,
Amid thy panoplied array,
  And gallant pomp around,
To meet thy last, decisive day,
When war, along the kindling fray,
  With dazzling horrors frowned;
While myriad swords around thee moved,
Flashing afar the blaze beloved;
And with thy name their battle cry,
The charging squadrons rushed to die.
But here, in Haup's inglorious swamp,
In subterrene, unwarlike camp,
The stones his pillow, and the reeds
The only couch he asks or needs,
A hero lay, whose sleepless soul
Was given, the spirits to control

Of lesser men; of heart as great
As thine, spoiled favourite of fate!
And he was wise, as bold and true,
To use the simple craft he knew;
  His skill from nature came;
A different clime, a different age,
Had scrolled his deeds in glory's page;
And proud as thine his wreath had been!
But if unlike thy closing scene,
  How more unlike thy fame!
Thy strife was for another's throne,
For realms and subjects not thine own,
  And for a conqueror's name:
He fought, because he would not yield
His birthright, and his fathers' field;
Would vindicate the deep disgrace,
The wrongs, the ruin of his race;—
He slew, that well avenged in death,
His kindred spirits pleased might be;—
Died, for his people and his faith,
His sceptre, and his liberty!

XII.

And on this night, whose parting shades
Shall see the avengers lift their blades,
And bring relentless fury, fraught
With many an insult's goading thought,
The outlaw SACHEM slept;
The while his scanty band around,
Low in the swamp's unequal ground,
Their mournful vigils kept.
Tall trees o'erthrown their bulwark made,
While rude, luxuriant vines o'erspread,
Concealed their lurking place;
There, now to feeble numbers worn,
In strength o'erspent, in hope forlorn,
Shrunk, trembling for the coming morn,
The WAMPANOAG race.

XIII.

Mothers and widows sad, were then
Hidden within that gloomy fen;
Left for a space, by war, to mourn
Each sacred bond asunder torn.

Perchance they thought of many a scene
Departed, to return no more;
How, when the hunter's toil was o'er,
And dressed his frugal meal had been,
His children clustered round his knee,
To hear the tales of former days,
And learn what men should strive to be,
While listening to the warrior's praise:
And she, thrice happy parent! sate,
Well pleased, beside her honoured mate;
What time gray eve its welcome hue
O'er distant hills and forests threw:
Nor idle then, with dexterous hand,
She wrought the glittering wampum band;
Or loved the silken grass to braid;
Or through the deer-skin, smooth and strong,
Weaving the many-coloured thong,
Her hunter's comely sandals made.
This they recalled; and marvelled they,
When bounteous earth is wide and free,
Why man, whose life is for a day,
So much in love with wo should be!

XIV.

He slept, yet not the spirit slept;
Her feverish vigil memory kept;
In motley visions on her eye,
The phantom host of dreams past by.
Tradition, meet for vulgar faith,
Has told of threats of coming skaith,
Spoke by the Evil One, who came,
This eve, his destined prey to claim,
In form, as when at noon of night,
He met him on the mountain's height:
O'er the gray rock the fiend outspread
His sable pinions as he fled,
And ere the sounding air he cleft,
His foot gigantic impress left.
Such superstition's idle tale,
But let the minstrel's lore prevail.

XV.

He saw the world of souls; and there,
Brave men and beauteous women were:

Fair forms to chiefs of godlike mien,
Reposing in their arbours green,
Supplied the spicy bowls they quaffed,
And round them danced, and joyous laughed;
While aye the warriors smiled to see
Those lovely creatures in their glee;
And pledged them in the sparkling cup;
Or breathed their fragrant incense up;
Grateful and pure, 'twas seen to flow
From calumets like stainless snow.
Apart reclined in kingly state,
The ancient MASSASOIET sate,
And earnest with UNCOMPOEN old,
Speech grave, but pleasant, seemed to hold;
Uncompoën, slain in recent fight,
Contending for his nephew's right.
Just from the woods, like hunter dight,
The gallant OUAMSUTTA came;
Bearing behind his plenteous game,
In order moved the warrior's train;
Joyous his bearing was, and free,

As if fatigue and wounds and pain,
In that blest world could never be;
His buskins trapped with glittering gold,
His floating mantle's graceful fold
Clasped with a sparkling gem;
Dazzling his cincture's radiance gleamed,
Woven from the heavenly bow it seemed,
And like the sunrays danced and streamed
  His feathery diadem.
A spear with silver tipt he bore;
The gaily-tinkling rings before,—
  The quiver rattling on his back,
His buoyant frame and kindling eye,
The thrilling pulse of transport high,
  The sense of power and pleasure spake.
And one and all the SACHEM knew,
When near their blissful bower he drew;
And clapped their hands with joy to see
The hero join their company.
And strains of softest music round,
From flutes and tabors, with the sound

Of voices, sweet as sweetest bird,
To greet the entering guest were heard.
" Welcome," they sung, " thy toils are done,
Thy battles fought, thy rest is won;
And welcome to the world thou art,
Where kindred souls shall never part;
Honour on earth shall valour have,
And joy with us attends the brave."

XVI.

That ravishing dream was rapt away,
Vanished the forms, the music died;
And changeful fancy's wayward sway
Visions of darker hue supplied.
O'er frozen plains he seemed to go,
Mid driving sleet, and bluiding snow.
Then Assawomsett's lake he knew,
And dim descried, the tempest through,
Apostate SAUSAMAN arise;
Stiff were his gory locks with ice,
  And mangled was his form;

It towered aloft, to giant size;
Fierce shone the fury of his eyes,
  Like lightning through the storm.
He cried, "My spirit hath no home!
A weary, wandering ghost, I roam.
This night the avengers lift the blade,
And my foul murder shall be paid!"

XVII.

Then thought the SACHEM that his way
Through Metapoiset's forest lay.
Mid the thick shadows of the grove,
  A form was rushing seen;
He saw with wildered paces rove
  Pocasset's warrior queen.
As from the water's depths she came,
With dripping locks and bloated frame.
Wild her discoloured arms she threw
To grasp him; and as swift he flew,
Her hollow scream he heard behind,
Come mingling with the howling wind.

"Why fly from Wetamoe? she died,
Bearing the war-axe on thy side!"

XVIII.

Now in a gloomy glade he stood;
Along the sward, the tracks of blood
Led, where in death a couguar lay;
Fast ebbed the crimson stream away;
But fiercely rolled his balls of fire,
And flashed their unextinguished ire
Toward the forest; where the chief
An armëd Indian could descry,
Who, less in anger than in grief,
Seëmed to behold his victim die,
Though lost his features were in gloom.
But Philip knew his hour was come,
And death from Indian hand was nigh.
For that red tiger oft had been,
In earlier dreams prophetic, seen.
It was the emblem of his soul,
The shade that still his life attended;

And but when life attained its goal,
He knew its visioned being ended.

XIX.

He woke, and from his covert sprung;
O'er the dark fen deep silence hung;
The moon had burst her sable shroud,
And from a silver-skirted cloud
Emerging, radiant but serene,
Looked forth upon the varying scene.
Now verging to the opening west,
  Her beams obliquely fell;
O'er the broad hill's rock-girdled breast,
  O'er thicket, glade and dell;
Scattered the bay's blue waters o'er,
And lit Pocasset's shelving shore.
'Twas as if now, when fate was near,
Awhile she brushed away her tear;
That, the last time, the SACHEM'S eye,
His native regions might descry,—
So lovely in that trembling beam,
That well his soul entranced might deem,

The Spirits' world, with all its bliss,
Had not a realm so fair as this.

XX.

If sorrow hath its feeling high,
And sadness its sublimity,
'Tis when the hero on his fate,
With thought composed, can meditate;
Throw o'er the past a steady eye,
And bid an ingrate world good-by!
Long and intently gazed the chief,
Till found his thoughts in speech relief.
"Like thee, fair Sun of night! have I,
Through mountain clouds of destiny,
Struggling, and darkened oft, been driven;
But fixed, as is thy course in heaven,
Nor brethren's fear, nor foeman's wrath,
Hath turned me from my purposed path.
My hour is come; my light is lost,
By never-bursting blackness crost;
While unrevenged my kindred lie,
My nation's ghosts indignant cry;

And unatoned, my native lands
Must captive pass to stranger hands.
But thou, in thine immortal march
Renewed, wilt span the eternal arch:
Here wilt thou pour thy mellow flood,
When other sandals press the sod:
Thou, eye of even! on yonder hill
Wilt look, serene and beauteous still,
When the last echo shall have died,
That spoke my tribe's expiring pride;
Thy quenchless font diminished not,
When METACOM shall be forgot.

XXI.

"Fair sun of night! thou movest alone;
Compeer or friend thou ne'er hast known,
Mid all the swarms in yonder plain,
That sparkle only in thy wane.
And lone as thine, my course has been,
Amid the multitudes of men.
Through all the crowds that hemmed me round,
My soul no kindred spirit found.

All brutish natures I could meet,
The wary, bold and strong and fleet;
But that, whereby men's spirits sway
The herds that fly them, or obey,
I could not waken to my will
Or touch to one responsive thrill;
The nobler powers of men unite,
In hopes, in council, or in fight.
Else, conquering ever, I had met
The foe I reverence, while I hate;
And to their ocean hurled agen
The intruders proud, who are but men.

XXII.

" I can believe what seers of old,
And earlier dreams have dimly told,—
With memory's casual beams, that play,
To mock with ineffectual ray,—
With those wild thoughts and fancies vain,
That idly cross the waking brain;—
I can believe some souls, that quit
Their fleshy forms, again are sent,—

Unconscious, after wanderings fit,
Of their forsaken tenement,—
By wisdom's lore to sway the host,
Or glow within a warrior's frame;
As thou, O moon! though sometimes lost,
Returnest, another, yet the same.
If thus it be,—or if the soul,
Escaped, shall wing its viewless flight,
Amid the clouds that o'er us roll,
To track the eagle's realms delight,
And swell the tempest's martial voice,
When spirits bold in fight rejoice;—
Or seek those far off western climes,
Whence came our sires, in distant times,
For ever with their shades to dwell;—
Where'er the spirit's course may be,
My last good-night I give to thee;
Since thou no more shalt beam on me,
Moon of my fathers! fare thee well!"

XXIII.

He heard soft steps advancing fast;
Long shades o'er the rough fen were cast;

Indians draw near; in moments brief,
YAMOYDEN stands before the chief.
"Brother, well met; if firm thou art,
  With me to stand or bleed;
If not, even as thou camest, depart,
  No doubtful aid we need.
For treacherous dogs have sought the foe,
And soon our secret haunt will show;
Uncertain to remain or fly,
Our hope is but like men to die."
"SACHEM, no doubtful faith is mine;
My heart, my hand, my friends are thine.
To life to bind me there is nought;
Like thine, my kindred all have sought
  The world where spirits go;
Like thine, a captive led, my wife
Leaves me a beggared half of life,
Hopeless to struggle with the strife
  Of roaring waves of wo.
No wingëd sorcerer, from the bed,
Where they lie fathoms deep, and dead,
  My perished hopes can bring;

No charmëd bough can find again
My cherished treasure's secret vein;
And no sweet songster's welcome voice
Can bid this widowed heart rejoice,
  Or tell of budding spring.
My tongue with thee hath known no wile;
I liked thee not when stained with guile,
And helpless innocence thy spoil:
And yet if thine the serpent stroke,
  And thine the serpent sting,
Thy foes did first each deed provoke,
And rattling indignation spoke
  Swift vengeance on the wing.
Nor e'er shall Indian say that I
Stood calm, in recreant baseness nigh,
To see the foul and senseless beast
On generous valour coldly feast;
Gorge on, with no remorseless pang,
Nor feel the venom, nor the fang."

XXIV.

" Brother, enough; our wrongs the same,
One be our fate, and one our fame!"

Abrupt their speech the SACHEM broke,
For conscience smote him as he spoke.
In that high moment of despair,
When kindred valour swore to share
The hour of peril and of death,
The secret wrong lay hid beneath;
The deadly wrong, unthought, untold,—
And all was hollow, false and cold!
"Rise, warriors rise!" the chieftain cried;
"Even here, on Haup's majestic side,
Yet be the white man's power defied!
Once more our native holds shall see
The Wampanoägs' martial glee;
Once more their echoes shall prolong
Our ancient, sacred, warrior song!"

XXV.

Emerging from the chequered sod,
From moving tree, from parting clod,
A hundred Indians rise;
As if a wizard's power had bade
The graves in throes give up their dead,

The potent spells of fear obeyed,
At which the pale moon overhead
  Shrunk fading from the skies!
Around the expecting warriors ran;
His martial dance the chief began;
With ponderous club the earth he stroke,
And thus his death-song wildly woke.

Philip's Death-Song.

XXVI.

1.

"Heard ye, among the murmuring trees,
The spirits' whispering in the breeze?
Mark! where along the moonlight glade,
Flits the wandering hero's shade!
Old and sage OOSAMEQUEN!
Seekest thou thy people's groves agen?
Wise and ancient Sagamore!
Warily his wrongs he bore;
But still his spirit o'er its hate
Brooding did deeply meditate;

Living, it lowered on their abodes,
Dying, curst the white men's gods!

2.

See ye not a frowning ghost?
Valiant son of valiant sire!
Alas! that thine was not the boast,
OUAMSUTTA! to expire,
As warriors love their life to yield,
With blood-stained arms, on battle field!
The stately beech is green in vain,
When dies at top its vital part;
Wrought in thy brain the victor's chain,
And withered all thy manly heart.
But let thy foemen, from thy hearse,
Hear, and dread thy dying curse!

3.

Along the mist-clad mountain's brow
The deer may course in transport now;
O'er his plains may bounding go,
Bold, the shaggy buffalo;
Now the gray moose may fearless fly;
For cold the valiant hunters lie!

Strong was their arm; their step was fleet;
Swift as the deer's their wingëd feet:
How oft in desperate conflict low
They laid the madly struggling foe;
How oft their grasp, with sinewy might,
Has staid the elk, in wildest flight!

4.

Say, have I left ye, champions brave,
Forgot, dishonoured in your grave?
Say, did your spirits call in vain,
On one unmindful of the slain?
Brothers, have I idly stood,
When rung your war-cry in the wood;
When crimson battle stains ye took,
Your quivers filled, and war-clubs shook?
Ye for my long remembrance speak,
Midnight fire, and midnight shriek!
Scalps, that my deadly vows made good!
Fields, where I quaffed the bowl of blood!"

XXVII.

But here no more our song must dwell,
While other chiefs look up the tale
Of their forefathers' deeds;
TIASK and TESPIQUIN began,
And through their sanguine annals ran,
The feuds and wars of many a clan,
Lost to the storied race of man,
Nor of them memory heeds:
Then, doomed to fall by guileful plan,
Long spoke the generous ANNAWAN.
Meantime YAMOYDEN stood aloof;
He heard a solemn, still reproof,
Demanding why the song of blood,
Ascending to the Christian's God,
To his late vows succeeds?

YAMOYDEN.

CANTO VI.

YAMOYDEN.

CANTO SIXTH.

WOMAN! blest partner of our joys and woes!
Even in the darkest hour of earthly ill,
Untarnished yet, thy fond affection glows,
Throbs with each pulse, and beats with every thrill!
Bright o'er the wasted scene, thou hoverest still,
Angel of comfort to the failing soul;
Undaunted by the tempest, wild and chill,
That pours its restless and disastrous roll,
O'er all that blooms below, with sad and hollow howl!

When sorrow rends the heart, when feverish pain
Wrings the hot drops of anguish from the brow,
To sooth the soul, to cool the burning brain,
O, who so welcome and so prompt as thou!
The battle's hurried scene and angry glow,—
The death-encircled pillow of distress,—
The lonely moments of secluded wo,—
Alike thy care and constancy confess,
Alike thy pitying hand, and fearless friendship bless!

Thee youthful fancy loves in aid to call;
Thence first invoked the sacred sisters were;
The form that holds the enthusiast's heart in thrall,
He, mid his bright creation, paints most fair;—
True,—in this earthly wilderness of care,—
As hunter's path the wilds and forests through;
And firm,—all fragile as thou art,—to bear
Life's dangerous billows,—as the light canoe,
That shoots, with all its freight, the impetuous rapid's flow.

Thee, Indians tell, the first of men to win,
Clomb long the vaulted heaven's unmeasured height:
And well their uncouth fable speaks therein
The worth even savage souls can never slight.
Tired with the chase, the hunter greets at night
Thy welcome smile, the balm of every wo;
Thy patient toil makes all his labours light;
And from his grave when friends and kindred go,
Thou weeping comest, the sweet sagamité to strow!

I.

Left to the troublous thoughts that rose
To bar her wearied frame's repose,
Sad Nora, in her guardians' care,
Had past, in penitence and prayer,

The hours, till evening round descended,
And forests, shores and waters blended,
  In her pale, misty light:
The tenants of the wigwam slept,
And silently their prisoner crept
  Forth in the doubtful night;
She gazed, with moist and wistful eye,
As now the moon, through clouds on high,
  Climbed near her central height;
The wind, careering o'er the sky,
Scattered the rack confusedly;
  One moment all was bright,
The next with shadows overspread;
And dark the forests waved their head;
And dark each scene that lay beneath
The inconstant heaven's uncertain wreath,
  Arose upon her sight.

II.

And now the hour was near, she knew,
When, to his love and promise true,

YAMOYDEN from the mount would speed,
To seek his desolated cot;
It was in vain she mused, and sought
The morning's dark events to read,
  That tore her thence away
From all she loved, in danger's hour,
And to the gloomy ruffians' power
  Consigned her child a prey.
She only saw her husband, reft
Of all that fate unkind had left,
Roam through the forest, lost and wild,
Calling on NORA and her child;—
And then she thought upon the brave,
Doomed with him to a common grave,
Whom yet her warning voice might save.

III.

Unconscious where her footsteps strayed,
She roved through many a darksome glade,
Till, far from the forsaken glen,
She knew her morning's road agen.

She marked it by a lonely mound,
Raised by the traveller's pious hand,
That told, in its deserted ground,
Slept the dead heroes of the land;
Dead, ere upon the verdant strand
The invader's hostile feet were found;
Now sleeping, nameless and alone,
Beneath that heap of rugged stone.
Onward through thick embowering wood,
  Her lonely journey sped;
Deep was the tangled solitude
  That round the wanderer spread.
Onward she went, till wild and rude,
The tempest burst, in wrathful mood,
  Careering o'er her head.
Withdrawn was now the silver ray;
The lightning's momentary play
  A ruddier splendour shed;
Then midnight blackness round was cast;
Nor longer could the path be traced,
  And roving wild she fled.

IV.

Yamoyden rushed in that same hour
Forth from his desolated bower.
Alas! that hearts thus close allied
Should struggle with the severing tide,
  So near, yet so remote!
Like sailors of some perished bark,
Struggling mid billows vexed and dark;
While howls so loud the storm's career,
Each others' screams they cannot hear,
  Nor catch one dying note;
While but a single wave disparts
Those gallant, lost and faithful hearts!

V.

Soon reason left her mind again;
There seemed a gulf of thoughts and pain
Roaring around her harassed brain,
  Where nought distinct arose;
She knew not why she wandered there,
Nor heard the sound that rent the air,
  Nor felt the tempest's throes.

It seemed as if, in murmurs nigh,
Throbbed on her ear some melody,
  She once had loved and sung;
And well-known voices whispered near,
Even to her darkling memory dear;
And then a moment thundered by
The elemental revelry,
  And deafening round her rung.
But when to consciousness once more
She waked, she marked the billows' roar,
With troubled hue and sullen dash,
Oft lit by the retiring flash.
The storm had ceased its maddening rage,
And on her clouded pilgrimage
  The moon was slowly riding;
High, mid the fringings of the storm,
She showed, half hid, her lucid form,
  The scene of tumult chiding.

VI.

New terror blanched her pallid brow,
When o'er her path a stranger crost,

With wildered air, and footsteps slow,
As one in moody musings lost.
It was a red man she espied,
  And, on her nearer view,
Her kind deliverer and her guide
  The trembling lady knew.
The bold Mohegan shrunk to see
So wan, so fair a form as she;
In white was robed her slender frame,
And needs, he thought, a spirit came;
A spirit more beautiful than e'er
Had visited this gloomy sphere.
Her tremulous voice dissolved his spell;
"Mysterious friend!" she cried, "O tell,
Since life thou gavest me, where are those,
My husband and my infant, where,—
Without whom life is hard to bear,
A prison house of many woes!
Why was I torn from home away?
At whose command,—and wherefore,—say."
"Such oft thy question," said the chief,
"Amid the darkness of thy grief.

Then vain my words to reach thine ear;
For it was closed; and I could hear
Thy converse with the spirits near.
Christian, than this I know no more,—
'Twas METACOM's command that bore
Thy child to Pawkanawkut's shore.
And thou with him had'st gone; but I
Sought from his feeble cause to fly,
And thought that through thyself, for me,
Peace with thy brethren there might be:
Nor other aim had then, to save
Thy form from bondage or the grave.
Of UNCAS' race am I, who ne'er
Aught heeded woman's idle tear.
But when thou didst, in thy despair,
Hang on me like a wild flower fair,
To the bleak cliffs of Haup that clings,—
When thou wast borne beneath my wings,
So lovely, helpless, wo-begone,—
Amid our ruthless band alone,—
A new-born gush of mercy stole,
Like a fresh dew, upon my soul:

Ay! though thy treacherous race I hate,
That melting pity lingers yet.
Beautiful Christian! I would die,
To spare thine heart one heavy sigh!
But this is idle; wouldest thou seek
News of YAMOYDEN?" "Speak! O speak!"
"I saw him, as his swift canoe,
Hours since, toward the mountain flew.
I marked him, through the mists and gloom;
I knew him by his eagle plume,
And by his woven mantle red;"
"And thou wilt serve me,—thou hast said?
O then conduct me there!
And I will call on heaven to shed
Its choicest blessings o'er thy head,
Even with my dying prayer."
"Fair Christian! to the mountain side,
Gladly thy footsteps I will guide;
But where thy husband lies below,
With METACOM, I cannot go.
Sad scenes will meet thine eyes,"—"No more!
Kind chieftain, bear me to the shore!"

VII.

His boat was nigh; its fragile side
Boldly the venturous wanderer tried;
Along they shot o'er the murmuring bay,
As they bore for the adverse bank away.
I guess it was a full strange sight,
To see in the track of the ghostly light,
The swarthy chief and the lady bright,
  O'er the heaving waves borne on;
While her white wan cheek and robe of white
  The pale ray played upon;
And above his dusky plumage shook;
Backward was flung his feathery cloak,
As his brawny arms were stretched to ply
The oars that made their shallop fly:—
I ween that he who had seen them ride,
As they rose in turn o'er the bellying tide,
Had deemed it a vision of olden time,
Of Afric wizard in faëry clime;
In durance dread, by sorceries dark,
Who wafted a lady in magic bark.

And all above, and around them, save
Where the quivering beam was on the wave,
Was dubious light, and shifting shade,
By clouds and mists and waters made:
The snowy foam on the billow lay,
Then sunk in the black abyss away;
The rack went scudding before the blast,
And its gloom o'er the bay came swift and past;
Flittingly gleamed the silvery streak,
On the waving hills and mountain peak;
But the star of love looked out in the west,
As if that lone lady's path she blest.

VIII.

Swift, where the midway current swept,
His pirogue's course AHAUTON kept;
And soon, upon the opposing shore,
They saw their skiff securely moor;
And NORA knelt upon the sand,
And blest her God's directing hand;
Then on their course they bent;

Tall rocks, in rude disorder piled,
Frowned o'er the bank sublimely wild;
Where fancy's eye, at dusky hour,
Might image citadel and tower.
And, o'er the margin where they hung,
The fir from frequent fissure sprung;
Here, bending as it strove to lave
Its branches in the passing wave;
There, perched on high, with solemn cone,
It stood, in gloomy pride, alone.

IX.

She marked them not; nor, farther still,
Succeeding to that broken hill,
  Where wide the landscape lay;
Nor paused they where an ancient wood,
In dark repose, and silent, stood;
Beyond its awful solitude,
  The twain pursued their way.
Now, by the margin of the cove,
In rugged, winding path they rove.

She only looked, where, broad and high,
Mount Haup arose in majesty;
Lifting, through forests brown, its head,
Where the gray cliffs their rampart spread;
Their moss-clad brows the chroniclers
Of time, for many a thousand years,
That here, unstoried, came and went;
Aloft they stood, like battlement
Of Spirit's castle; as if there,
The wandering hosts of upper air,
In fleecy vapour oft revealed,
Nightly their spectral wassail held.

X.

And now, through wet and tangled ground,
Their pathway to the mountain wound.
The moon's last rays were trembling o'er
The hill, the bay, and adverse shore.
A moment, faintly bright, they rest
Upon the summit's naked breast;
Chequer the thickets on its side,
Shed filmy lines along the tide;

On distant bank and rock and isle,
Gleam with their melancholy smile;
They tip the farthest hills that bound
The fading landscape glimmering round;
Fringe the deep clouds with parting light,
Then fail, and all is lost in night.

XI.

In darkness and in doubt, they tried
The rising mountain's rugged side;
Rude and uneasy its ascent,
To one with toil and grief o'erspent.
She heard the startled fox's cry,
Pass with its sudden wailing nigh;
The wolf's sad howl came frequent by;
But human voice was heard not there;
'Twas lone and mournful as despair;—
No watchfire shot its gleams afar,
Nor woke the red man's song of war;—
If warriors in these shades reposed,
All was in utter silence closed.

XII.

Past is the long and rocky slope;
She stands upon the mountain top;
And cool is now the breeze that flings
O'er the bleak height its humid wings,
Freshening across the eastern bay,
The signal of approaching day.
And faintly, in the distant sky,
A gray beam stole on NORA's eye;
Dimly morn's struggling herald kist
The foldings of the billowy mist,
And fell upon the waves below,
With soft and melancholy glow.

XIII.

Here the MOHEGAN paused; he bent
Northward, awhile, his gaze intent;
As if he marked, mid glooms below,
The haunts where lay ensnared his foe.
Troubled he seemed, as one who doth
A task, to which his will is loath,

But feels some fatal power control,
As with resistless whirl, the soul.
" Christian," he cried, " I leave thee here,
Where danger's course thou need'st not fear.
He, who my brother slew, lies there!
And it were shame beyond repair,
If any but my father's son,
The murderer's scalp in battle won!
I would the tempest, o'er him spread,
Might burst but on the guilty head;
But the red bolt, once launched, must fall
In wrath and ruin upon all.
I go; but when the strife is past,
And the proud king lies cold at last,
When the foul birds shall downward sweep,
And forth the wolves on carnage peep,
Then may'st thou hence descend, to save
With thy sweet prayers the captive brave;
Bid the stained hand of slaughter stay
The axe impending o'er its prey;
Perchance YAMOYDEN rescue,—nay!
Now, vain thy farther journeying were.

Farewell! I leave thee thus alone,
But when my destined work is done,
His life shall be my dearest care."

XIV.

Silent and swift the chief departed;
Dark o'er the bosom of the hill,
Along the rocks she marked him steal,
Then in the thicket's depths he darted;
And she was left, alone to feel
The sad impatience that would see
The measure of its misery;
That hath, in man, nor hope nor friend,
Nor knows what time its wo shall end.
Then fervently the lone one prayed,
In this her trying hour, for aid.

XV.

Sad rose the morning; not in bloom
Awakening radiant from the gloom;
All nature gladdening as it spread,
And light and life, and glory shed;

Not sporting on the gentle gale,
That floats o'er stream and dewy vale;
Not bursting mid the kindling heaven,
Its hues in gold and purple given;—
For now, in dreary twilight lay
The scene beneath its mantle gray;
Mute was the melody of morn,
And hushed was nature's harp forlorn.
Alone, above the vaporous clouds,
That hung, with mournful hue, like shrouds,
  O'er every distant peak,
Rose a faint line, as morning here
Thro' the dark hosts her flag would rear,
  The coming day to speak.
Purple it seemed, yet lost and blending,
With the dull hues around ascending;
And a soft roseate tint was seen,
At intervals, the shades between;
As changeful, as unfixed it spread,
As the last bloom, ere life has fled.
But as the light of day uprose,
Those transient tints of beauty close;

In volumes dense, o'er earth and main,
Descend the wreathing mists again;
Pocasset's long and verdant coast
In that unwelcome veil was lost,
With sweep of hills and forests wide,
And sparkling waves between that glide;
Where, glancing o'er the sunny isles,
That stud the water's dimpling smiles,
The eye might ocean's breast explore,
Or scan the western streams that pour
Their tides on Narraganset's shore;
Or upward, to Patuxet's side,
Extend the tribute of their pride.
But now the scene had narrow bound,
And scarce the mountain's base beyond,
  Was aught distinctly seen:
Strange were the shapes that seemed to rise
Imperfectly upon the eyes;
And wildered fancy here might form
The awful Spirit of the storm,
  In all his terrors drest;

Stretching his giant arms abroad,
And throned where footsteps never trod;
Or high in gloomy car upborne,
Rushing to combat with the morn,
Upon the tempest's breast.

XVI.

Still as she gazed with anxious eye,
The expected battle to descry,
The breeze with murmurs low that sighed,
Came freshening from the eastern tide,
And swept the brooding mists away,
That o'er the northern prospect lay.
Rocks, woods and swamps arose to view,
Though yet o'erhung with vapoury hue;
And eastward, dimly mid the trees,
The English form and arms she sees;
Low couched beneath the forest shade,
Round lay their silent ambuscade.
Prostrate the moveless band she spied;
An Indian by a whiteman's side,

Alternate placed, was crouching seen,
Skirting the borders of the fen.

XVII.

Intently as she gazed, agen,
Elsewhere, she marked where armëd men
Westward were hid, in ambush close,
From where a swelling upland rose.
That knoll a practised eye alone
The haunt of savages had known;
For the rude sconce, around it reared,
Like thicket's tangled growth appeared.
And there the remnant of that race,
So long devoted to the chase,
Lay hid; thus hemmed, all unaware
What morning greetings foes prepare;—
But, as the elks in northern wood,
Girt by the hunter's circle fly,
And headlong plunging in the flood
New dangers meet, and with their blood
Staining the guarded waters, die;

So, vainly may the band betrayed
Rush from their leaguered palisade,
The swamp's recesses dark to try,—
There, too, relentless foemen lie.

XVIII.

As Nora marked them, from the knoll,
With wary steps an Indian stole;
And seemed it, that the thicket's screen
Kept from his glance the foe unseen.
For forth he gazed; and though in sad
And dusky livery morn was clad,
Nature's free kingdom seemed to yield
A transport through his heart that thrilled.
He leapt for joyance; when a flame
Bright from the ambushed thicket came;
The death-ball whizzed, with angry knell,
And from the rampart wild he fell.

XIX.

Then, as that signal's echoes rung,
Far flashed the fire, the woods among.

Too soon their shot the ambush sent;
Innocuous o'er the foe it went.
But the dun smoke that upward flew,
The fortress veiled from NORA's view,
Till, as the breezes slowly bear
Its volumes through the drizzly air,
She marked the assaulted Indians glide
Forth from their bulwark's eastward side,—
Unclosed, that timely they might gain
The marsh;—disordered ran the train;
The dark morass they hurried through,
Ever low-bending, as they flew,
Where sinking soil, and bush and tree,
Might best their screen and shelter be.
And issuing from the forest's verge,
Swift on their track the foemen urge;
As beagles to the death-scent true,
They rushed, and as remorseless too;—
The English, for their brethren's blood,—
Mohegans, for their ancient feud,—
Seaconets, too, by treachery base,
Who hoped to win the conquerors' grace;—

How weak the web that treason wove,
When ruin followed if it throve!

XX.

Then rose from that wild swamp the shout
That followed on the Indians' rout;
And their mad yell of fear and wrath,
As the shot whistled o'er their path;
And flame and smoke, far scattering, met
The lady's glance, who lingered yet
Above;—but then a film came o'er
Her sight, and she beheld no more.
A husband's death-cry in her ear
Came sadly, wildly ringing near;
And from the mountain steep she sped,
Unknowing where her pathway led.

XXI.

With that abrupt and steep descent,
Her senses reeled, her breath was spent;
But she was borne, in her giddy way,
To where the eastern ambush lay.

They marked her not, though near she came;
Fixed was their gaze, intent their aim,
Where, lost in their uncertain dread,
A band confused of Indians fled,
  Toward the forest bound;
Quick paused they in their progress rash,
The thicket kindled with the flash,
  And rung the musket sound.
Staggered, dismayed, the wildered band;
Some idly drew, with trembling hand,
Their moose-strings wet; the forest through
The arrowy shower in mockery flew;
A few their deadlier arms employ,
But now as powerless to destroy;
Then scattering, as the allied force
Uprose and urged upon their course,
  Swift o'er the fen they fly;
Yet Nora heard, above the rout,
The volleying shot and scream and shout,
  Old Annawan's war-cry.
He strove, with cheer, reproach and threat,
His naked band to rally yet,

And yet the unequal conflict wage;
But vain, stout heart! thy gallant rage,
That well, on this sad field, became
The trophies of thine ancient fame!

XXII.

Thus from the covert where she stood,
Vanished the motley multitude;
One only here erect remained,
And moveless; one alone disdained
To gnaw the toils his hunters spread,
But reared at bay his monarch head.
A white man and an Indian near,
Fronted and staid his bold career;
And scarce their muskets' length apart,
Stood, levelling at the warrior's heart.
Thus stopt he, barred in his advance;
Firm on the twain he fixed his eye,
Fierce as the pouncing falcon's glance;
His battle-axe he brandished high;
Else all unarmed. An instant there
Paused in their purposed work the pair;

So proud, in his defenceless state,
And terrible, he seemed to wait,
Himself to death to dedicate!
Trembling, the white man first gave fire,
But saw in faithless flash expire
  The engine's fatal store;
" Thine is the chance the prize to gain,"—
  He said, but spoke no more,
Ere, hurled with dexterous hand amain,
Sunk the fell tomahawk in his brain,
And down, a ghastly corse, he fell!
Then strait a loud and joyous yell
  His Indian comrade gave:
" A ghost had been incensed," he cried,
" If thou by other arm had'st died!
  This, from his gory grave,
Sends Agamoun!" he said, and true,
On their swift wings, the death balls flew.
A moment yet the Sachem stood,
His right hand planted on his breast,
Where inward gushed the vital blood
And his attempted words suppress.

AHAUTON marked his dying look,
Speaking its stern and sad rebuke;
Then in the moor's dank, miry bed,
Deep fell the indignant chieftain, dead!

XXIII.

This in a moment's space was past;
But as around the wanderer cast
  Her gaze, a vision came,
That drew, despite of toil and fear,
Even to the verge of battle near
  Her now exhausted frame.
Amid a roving band, alone,
Her father in the fen was thrown,
Now feeble waxed with age and toil;
And scarce upon the slippery soil
He kept his footing; while he held,
With strength surpassing that of eld,
  The ruffian host at bay;
A well-known voice salutes her ear,
Even in that hurried scene most dear;

A well-known form she marked among
That haggard, fierce and desperate throng,
Round, howling for their prey;
And, o'er her father's white hairs swung,
As high a murderous axe was hung,
She saw YAMOYDEN stay
The lifted arm; alas! too late
To break the blow, impelled by fate!
Averted from the old man's head,
On his own faithful breast it fell!
A rescue comes,—the Indians fled,—
Far off the sounds of conflict swell;—
But never more, on battle field,
That valiant arm shall weapon wield;
Nor, mid the combat's voices blending,
His cheering cry be heard ascending!

XXIV.

Dying he lay; and o'er him bent
FITZGERALD, now with kind intent.
As ebbed the living current fleet,
He whispered soothing comfort sweet,

Fraught with such heavenly nourishment,
Such chrism to the departing soul,
As amber gum to feverish vein;
Deep in the mental wound it stole,
Forgotten then his mortal pain.
What form comes floating on his glance,
Brightest in that celestial trance?
"Fair image of my blessëd wife!
Comest thou too, from the load of life
To loose the spirit's struggling wing,
And bid it upward, upward spring?
Wilt thou not join me in that clime,
On whose far shore the waves of time
Fall with faint murmur as they flow?—
Our child—farewell!"—"YAMOYDEN, no!
Alone thy spirit will not go.
We have not loved as those that woo,
Amid the spring-tide's laughing flowers,
And in green summer only true,
Part ere dark winter's chilling hours.
Hearts, long in grief and danger tried,
Relenting death will ne'er divide!"

XXV.

Thus faintly murmuring, by his side
Exhausted sunk his faithful bride.
She strove, with her long locks unbound,
To stanch the grim and ghastly wound;
Her husband's arms, with dying grasp,
Her lovely, wasted form enclasp;
Her constant bosom to his breast
Closer and closer still he prest;
Her gaze met his, where every ray
Of earthly passion past away;
The glance of love, that conquers time,
Was blent with confidence sublime;
As if on their departing view,
With heaven, that love was opening too!
Fitzgerald, bending o'er them, brushed
Aside the tears that freely gushed.
"Farewell, misguided one!" he said,—
"Dim light along thy path was shed;
There may be mercy, even for thee!
Thy child is safe; may heaven to me
Be kind as I to him shall be!

May this thy parting hour be sweet;
  Thy wounded conscience healed;
With unction of the Paraclete,
  Thy soul's salvation sealed;
And may thy parted spirit meet
  Thy Saviour's form revealed.

XXVI.

The old man's glance was heavenward cast,
As breathed that wish, the best, the last,
And strong and fervent was his prayer,
Communing with his Father there.
He viewed them as they lay reclined,
Their lips conjoint, their forms entwined.
They moved not, heaved not, breathed not, yet
It seemed the lovers' glances met.
He knelt, he strove his child to raise,
But vain the task the sire essays;
He felt no struggle; caught no sound;
But to each other they were bound,
So close, that vain were all endeavour,
With aught that sacred clasp to sever,

Save sacrilegious knife ;
The father gazed in anguish wild,—
He prest the bosom of his child,—
There beat no pulse of life !

CONCLUSION.

Sad was the theme, which yet to try we chose,
In pleasant moments of communion sweet;
When least we thought of earth's unvarnished
woes,
And least we dreamed, in fancy's fond deceit,
That either the cold grasp of death should meet,
Till after many years, in ripe old age;
Three little summers flew on pinions fleet,
And thou art living but in memory's page,
And earth seems all to me a worthless pilgrimage.

Sad was our theme; but well the wise man sung,
"Better than festal halls, the house of wo;"
Tis good to stand destruction's spoils among,
And muse on that sad bourne to which we go.
The heart grows better when tears freely flow;
And, in the many-coloured dream of earth,
One stolen hour, wherein ourselves we know,

Our weakness and our vanity,—is worth
Years of unmeaning smiles, and lewd, obstreperous
mirth.

'Tis good to muse on nations passed away,
For ever, from the land we call our own;
Nations, as proud and mighty in their day,
Who deemed that everlasting was their throne.
An age went by, and they no more were known!
Sublimer sadness will the mind control,
Listening time's deep and melancholy moan;
And meaner griefs will less disturb the soul;
And human pride falls low, at human grandeur's
goal.

PHILIP! farewell! thee KING, in idle jest,
Thy persecutors named; and if in deed,
The jewelled diadem thy front had prest,
It had become *thee* better, than the breed
Of palaces, to sceptres that succeed,
To be of courtier or of priest the tool,
Satiate dull sense, or count the frequent bead,

Or pamper gormand hunger; thou wouldest rule
Better than the worn rake, the glutton or the fool!

I would not wrong thy warrior shade, could I
Aught in my verse or make or mar thy fame;
As the light carol of a bird flown by,
Will pass the youthful strain that breathed thy
name:
But in that land whence thy destroyers came,
A sacred bard thy champion shall be found;
He of the laureate wreath for thee shall claim
The hero's honours, to earth's farthest bound,
Where Albion's tongue is heard, or Albion's songs
resound.

NOTES.

NOTES TO CANTO FIRST.

STANZA II.

The forest cinctured mountain stood.

Mount Hope appears to have been called by the Indians Mont Haup, or Montaup; and has been thence easily corrupted into its present name. It has given occasion for many pleasant puns to Mr. Hubbard and Cotton Mather. As when Philip fled there, in his last exigency, it is called Mount Hope, rather Mount Misery—"lucus a non lucendo," &c. It is called Haup, throughout the poem; improperly, I believe—Transeat cum cæteris. The following description is pretty correct; although somebody has been playing a hoax upon the worthy meditator among the tombs; first, as to the name of the hill; secondly, as to the fact of Philip's choosing the most conspicuous situation he could possibly select, when he most needed concealment; and, thirdly, as to the circumstance of his droll exhibition, on the occasion of his death. That there is no foundation for this tradition seems evident, from the account of Captain Church himself, extracted in the Notes to the Sixth Canto.

"King Philip, as he is usually called, erected his wigwam on a lofty and beautiful rise of land in the eastern part of Bristol, which is generally known by the name of Mount Hope. According to authentic tradition, however, *Mon Top* was the genuine aboriginal name of this celebrated eminence. To this there was, no doubt, an appropriate meaning; but it cannot, at present, be easily ascertained.

"From the summit of this mount, which is, perhaps, less than three hundred feet* above high water mark, it is said, that in a

* By a late admeasurement it is not much more than two hundred.

clear day, every town in Rhode-Island may be seen. The towering spires of Providence in one direction, those of Newport in another, the charming village of Bristol, the fertile island of Poppasquash, fields clothed with a luxuriant verdure as far as the eye can stretch, irregular meandering waters intersecting the region to the west, Mount Hope bay on the east, and distant lands, with various marks of high cultivation, form, in the aggregate, a scene truly beautiful and romantic.

"The late Lieut. Gov. Bradford, in early life, knew an aged squaw, who was one of Philip's tribe, was well acquainted with this Sagamore in her youthful days, and had often been in his wigwam. The information through her is, therefore, very direct as to the identical spot where he fixed his abode. It was a few steps south of Captain James De Wolf's summer-house, near the brow of the hill, but no vestige of the wigwam remains. The eastern side of this hill is very steep, vastly more so than that at Horse Neck, down which the intrepid Putnam trotted his sure-footed steed, in manner worthy of a knight of the tenth century, *in time of the revolutionary war*, and wonderfully escaped his pursuing enemy.

"When Church's men were about to rush upon Philip, he is said to have evaded them by springing from his wigwam, as they were entering it, and rolling, like a hogshead, down the precipice which looks towards the bay.

"Having reached the lower part of this frightful ledge of rocks, without breaking his bones, he got upon his feet and ran along the shore, in a northeasterly direction, about a hundred rods, and endeavoured to screen himself in a swamp, then a quagmire, but now terra firma.

"Here the Sachem of Mon Top, long the Magormissabib of the New-England colonies, was shot, on the 12th of August, 1676, by Richard,* one of his Indians, who had been taken, a little before, by the noted Captain Church, and was become his friend and soldier.

"The ledge of rocks, forming the precipice before mentioned, extends, for a considerable distance, nearly parallel with the shore of the bay. In a certain situation between the site of the wigwam

* This was not his name;—See the Notes to Canto VI.

and the place where Philip received his death wound, and where the solid mass of quartz, which forms the basis of Mon Top, is nearly perpendicular and forty or fifty feet high, is a natural excavation of sufficient dimensions to afford a convenient seat. It is five or six feet from the ground, and is known by the name of Philip's *Throne.* A handsome grass plat of small extent lies before it. At the foot of the throne is a remarkably fine spring of water, from which proceeds a never-failing stream. This is called Philip's Spring.

" On that throne, tradition says, Philip used often to sit in regal style, his warriors forming a semicircle before him, and give law to his nation."—*Rev. T. Alden's collection of Epitaphs.* Pentade I. Vol. IV.

Aquetnet green.

Aquetnet was the Indian name for the island, now called Rhode-Island.—*New-England's Memorial,* 116.

Pocasset's Hills.

The Pocasset shore, now called Tiverton, is opposite Mount Hope.

STANZA IV.

Now two score years of peace had past, &c.

" As for the rest of the Indians, ever since the suppression of the Pequods, in the year 1637, until the year 1675, there was always in appearance amity and good correspondence on all sides; scarce an Englishman was ever known to be assaulted or hurt by any of them until after the year 1674, &c."—*Hubbard's Narrative of the Indian Wars in New-England, &c.*

Until the Pequods' empire fell.

" The Pequots, or Pequods, were a people seated in the most southerly bounds of New-England; whose country the English of Connecticut jurisdiction doth now, for the most part, possess. This nation were a very warlike and potent people, about forty years since: at which time they were in their meridian. Their chief Sachem held dominion over divers petty Sagamores; as over part of Long-Island, over the Mohegans, and over the Sagamores of Quinapeake, yea over all the people that dwelt upon Connecticut river, and over some of the most southerly inhabitants of the Nipmuck country, about Quinabaag. The principal Sachem lived at, or about Pequot, now called Lew-London. These Pequots, as old Indians relate, could, in former times, raise four thousand men fit for war; and held hostility with their neighbours, that lived bordering upon them to the east and north, called the Narragansitts or Nechegansitts; but now they are few, not above three hundred men; being made subject unto the English, who conquered and destroyed most of them, upon their insolent deportment and just provocation, Anno 1638."—*Gookin's Historical Collections of the Indians in New-England; first printed from the original manuscript, at Boston, in* 1792.

" Historians have treated of the Pequots and Moheagans as two distinct tribes, and have described the Pequot country, as lying principally within the three towns of New-London, Groton and Kensington. All the tract above this, as far north and east as has been described, they have represented as the Moheagan country. Most of the towns in this tract, if not all of them, hold their lands by virtue of deeds from Uncas, or his successors, the Moheagan Sachems. It is, however, much to be doubted, whether the Moheagans were a distinct nation from the Pequots. They appear to have been a part of the same nation, named from the place of their situation. Uncas was evidently of the royal line of the Pequots, both by his father and mother; and his wife was daughter of Tatobam, one of the Pequot Sachems. He appears to have been a petty Sachem, under Sassacus, the great prince of the nation. When the English first came to Connecticut, he was in a state of rebellion against him, and of little consequence among the Indians. The Pequots were, by far, the most warlike nation in Connecticut, or even in New-England, &c. Their principal fort was on a commanding and most beautiful eminence, in the town of Groton, a few miles southeasterly from Fort Griswold. This was the royal fortress, where the chief Sachem had his residence. He had another fort near Mystic river, a few miles to the eastward of this, called Mystic fort. The Pequots, Moheagans and Nehantics, could doubtless muster a thousand bowmen."—*Trumbull's History of Connecticut*, I. p. 42.

" The *Mahiccanni*," says Mr. Heckewelder, " have been called by so many names, that I was at a loss which to adopt, so that the reader might know what people were meant. Lookiel calls them 'Mohicans,' which is nearest to their real name Mahiccanni, which, of course, I have adopted. The Dutch called them Mahicanders; the French Mourigans, and Mahingans; the English, Mohiccons, Mohuccans, Mohegans, Muhheekanew, Schaticooks, River Indians."

They are called Muhhekaneews, by Dr. Edwards, in his "*Observations*" on their language, published at New-York, 1801. The old historians of New-England term them Moheags, Moheaks and Mohegins, &c. I have adopted in the text the mode of writing it which seemed most euphonious. These people were one of the most martial and important tribes of the great family to which the Delawares belonged, called *Lenopi* by Mr. Jefferson, in his "Notes on Virginia," and *Lenni Lenape,** by Mr. Heckewelder. The latter author agrees with the venerable historian of Connecticut, as to the Mohicans being the same race with the Pequods.

Until the Pequots' empire fell, &c.

I have thought it necessary to make the foregoing extracts, in relation to the people, who, after their decisive overthrow, mentioned in the text, always took part with the English against Philip. But as the events recapitulated in the fourth and six following stanzas, were merely premised, as explanatory of the allusions made in the poem, it is unnecessary to give much more than references to the authors who have recorded them.

And Sassacous, &c.

The name of the Pequod Sagamore is thus written, without the diæresis, by the Rev. Mr. Hubbard. The accent is, however, placed on the first syllable, in a poem by Gov. Winthrop, preserved in the "*Collections of the Massachusetts Historical Society.*" "At Sassacus' dread name," &c.

The Pequods quarrelled with the colonists at an early period of the settlement; and, after a hollow treaty of peace, which they entered into, in the year 1636, they protected certain of the Narragansetts who had murdered some of the English on Block-Island. This led to a war, in the course of which the Narragansetts, with the versatile and jealous policy of Indian nations, made their own

---

* Meaning, an original people. αυτοχθονες.

peace with the English, and refused to assist the Pequots. They appear, however, to have experienced some compunction when the Pequod fort was attacked by the English, on the 26th May, 1637; when, after a vigorous and desperate resistance by the savages, the fort was fired by Captain Mason's men, sixty or seventy wigwams burnt, and seven hundred of the miserable Pequods destroyed. The Narragansetts were mere spectators on this occasion. They either felt, or pretended, an unconquerable fear of Sassacus, whom they called invincible; saying, "he was all one god." Uncas, Sachem of the Mohegans, who, as has been already mentioned, was in a state of revolt against the great Sagamore when the English first settled in Connecticut, was their guide to the fortress of his enemy; and ever after, with wary and more consistent policy than belonged to his brethren, adhered to the interests of his new allies. Sassacus fled to the Mohocks, (termed Mohogs and Maquas* by the old historians,) who murdered him and sent his scalp to the conquerors. —*See Trumbull's History of Connecticut, and the authorities there quoted; also Hubbard's Narrative of the troubles with the Indians, first published, by authority, at Boston,* 1677. *New-England's Memorial, Boston printed, Newport reprinted,* 1777. *Prince's Chronological History of New-England, Boston,* 1736. *Mather's Magnalia, Book VII. &c.*

Till Metacom his war-dance held.

"The Paukanawkutts were a great people heretofore. They lived to the east and northeast of the Narragansitts; and their chief Sachem held dominion over divers other petty Sagamores, upon the island of Nantuckett, and Nope, or Martha's Vineyard, of Nawsett, of Mannamoyk, of Sawkattukett, Nobsquasitt, Matakees and several others, and some of the Nipmucks. Their country, for the most part, falls within the jurisdiction of New-Plymouth colony. This people were a potent nation in former times; and could raise, as the most credible and ancient Indians affirm, about three thousand men. They held war with the Narragansitts, &c. This

---

* *Maqua*, in the Mohegan tongue, which is the same with the Chippeway and Algonquin, means *Bear*. See the vocabularies in Dr. Edwards' 'Observations.' 'Carver's Travels' and the Appendix to Baron Le Hontan. So, *Mahingan* means a *Wolf*; and their tribe was called *Les Loups* by the French, according to Mr. Jefferson.

nation, a very great number of them were swept away by an epidemical and unwonted sickness, An. 1612 and 1613, about seven or eight years before the English arrived in those parts, to settle the colony of New-Plimouth. Thereby Divine Providence made way for the peaceable and quiet settlement of the English in those nations. What this disease was, that so generally and mortally swept away, not only those, but other Indians, their neighbours, I cannot well learn. Doubtless it was some pestilential disease. I have discoursed with some old Indians, that were then youths; who say, that the bodies all over were exceeding yellow, describing it by a yellow garment they showed me, both before they died, and afterward." —*Gookin.*

Of this people, the Wampanoags, or Wampanoogs, &c. (as it is differently written,) seem to have been the immediate clan or family of old Massasoit, or Massasoiet, or Woosamequen,* the father of Metacom, or Metacomet,† called King Philip by the English. The latter, however, signs his treaties, "Philip, Sachem of Pokanoket, his mark, P."

"When Plimouth Colony was first planted, within three monettes after their first landing, March 16, 1620, Massasoit, the chief Sachem of all that side of the country, repaired to the English at Plymouth, and entred into a solemn League upon sundry Articles, printed in N. E. Memorial, 1669, p. 24. The words are as followeth," &c.—*Hubbard, Old Edition* 7. *Edition of* 1814, p. 56.

"The which League the same Sachim, Sept. 25, 1630,‡ a little before his death, coming with his eldest son [*Mooanam or Wamsutta*] afterward called Alexander, did renew with the English at the Court of Plimouth, for himself and his Son, and their Heirs and Successors; and after that he came to Mr. Brown's, that lived not far from Mount Hope, bringing his two Sons, Alexander and

* The Indians were in the habit of changing their names, at their great war dances. Thus, Canonchet was afterwards called Nanunteno.

† Printed, I suppose, by mistake, *Metamocet*, in the Analectic Magazine, containing the life of Philip, by Mr. Irving. See *Increase Mather's Brief History of the Warr, &c. Boston*, 1676.

‡ Should be 1639, as Hubbard has it himself in the next page, and as it is in N. E. Memorial. The error is not corrected in the new edition of Hubbard.

Philip, with him, desiring that there might be Love and Amity after his death, between his Sons and them, as there had been betwixt himself and them in former times: yet it is very remarkable, that this Massasoit, called also Woosamequen (how much soever he affected the English, yet) was never in the least degree any wayes well affected to the religion of the English, but would have had them engaged never to attempt to draw away any of his people, from their old Pagan Superstition and devilish Idolatry," &c. —*Idem.*

" After the death of this Woosamequen or Massasoit, [about 1656,] his eldest son succeeded him about twenty years since, Alexander by name, who, notwithstanding the league he had entred into with the English, together with his father, in the year 1639, had neither affection to the Englishmen's persons, nor yet to their religion, but had been plotting with the Narhagansets to rise against the English, of which the Governour and Council of Plimouth being informed, they presently sent for him to bring him to the Court; the person to whom that service was committed, was a prudent and resolute gentleman, the present Governour of the said Colony, who was neither afraid of danger, nor yet willing to delay in a matter of that moment. He forthwith, taking eight or ten stout men with him well armed, intended to have gone to the said Alexander's dwelling, distant at least forty miles from the Governour's house, but by a good providence he found him whom he went to seek at an Hunting House, within six miles of the English Towns, where the said Alexander, with about eighty men, were newly come in from hunting, and had left their guns without doors, which Major Winslow, with his small company, wisely seized, and conveyed away, and then went into the wigwam, and demanded Alexander to go along with him before the Governour, at which message he was much appalled, but being told by the undaunted Messenger, that if he stirrd or refused to go he was a dead man; he was by one of his chief Counsellors, in whose advise he most confided, perswaded to go along to the Governour's house, but such was the pride and height of his spirit, that the very surprizal of him, raised his choler and indignation, that it put him into a feaver, which, notwithstanding all possible means that could be used, seemed Mortal; whereupon intreating those that held him prisoner, that he might have liberty to return home, promising to return again if he recovered, and to send his son as hostage till he could do so; on that consideration he was fairly dismissed, but dyed before he got half way home."—*Idem.* Our author then makes a sort of apology, for the treatment of Alexander. He says it was never urged as a cause of offence, by the said Alexander's brother, by name Philip, commonly for his ambitious and haughty spirit nicknamed King Philip. Nothing, he says, could have induced the said Philip to make war on the English, "besides the instigation of Satan, that either envied at the prosperity of the Church of God here seated, or else fearing lest the power of the Lord Jesus, that had overthrown his Kingdome in other parts of the World, should do the like here, and so the stone taken out of the Mountain without hands, should become a great mountain itself, and fill the whole earth, no cause of provocation being given by the English."

Thus died, of a broken heart, the proud-spirited brother of Philip. Cotton Mather, who treats the Netops, as he calls them, with very little ceremony, condescends to mention, that "Alexander was treated with no other than that *humanity* and *civility*, which was always *essential* to the Major General; nevertheless, the *inward fury* of his own guilty and haughty mind threw him into such a *fever* as cost him his life." *Magnalia. Book VII. Ecclesianum prœlia, or the wars of the Lord,* p. 45. a. and b.

To him succeeded Metacom, or King Philip, Anno 1662; "who," as the learned, but quaint, Annalist goes on to state, "after he had solemnly renewed his *covenant* of *Peace* with the English, most perfidiously broke it by making an attempt of war upon them in the year 1671, wherein being seasonably and effectually defeated, he humbly confessed his breach of *covenant*, and subscribed articles of *submission*, &c. Indeed, when the Duke of *Archette*, at his being made Governour of *Antwerpe* Castle, took an oath to keep it faithfully for King *Philip* of *Spain;* the officer that gave him his oath used these odd words, *If you perform what you promise, God help you; if you do it not, the Devil take you body and soul!* And all the standers by cried, *Amen.* But when the Indian King *Philip* took an oath to be faithful unto the Government of *New-England* no body used *these words* unto him; nevertheless, you shall anon see whether *these words* were not expressive enough of what became of him!"—*Idem*, p. 45. b.

It would be too troublesome, as well as unnecessary, to give even a sketch of the life of Philip, up to the time when the Poem commences. A connected account of the Sachem's adventures may be found in *Mather's Magnalia*, *Increase Mather's Brief History*, &c. *Hutchinson's History of Massachusetts*, vol. I. and *Trumbull's History of Connecticut*, vol. I. The following note in *Holmes's American Annals*, does justice to his character, and makes proper allowance for the measures taken by the English.

"The death of Philip, in retrospect, makes different impressions from what were made at the time of the event. It was then considered as the extinction of a virulent and implacable enemy; it is now viewed as the fall of a great warrior, a penetrating statesman, and a mighty prince. It then excited universal joy and congratulation, as a prelude to the close of a merciless war; it now awakens sober reflections on the instability of empire, the peculiar destiny of the aboriginal race, and the inscrutable decrees of Heaven. The patriotism of the man was then overlooked in the cruelty of the savage; and little allowance was made for the natural jealousy of the sovereign, on account of the barbarities of the warrior. Philip, in the progress of the English settlements, foresaw the loss of his territory, and the extinction of his tribe; and made one mighty effort to prevent those calamities. Our pity for his misfortunes would be still heightened, could we entirely rely on the tradition, (mentioned by Callender, 73.) that Philip and his chief old men, were at first averse to the war; that Philip wept with grief, at the news of the first English who were killed; and that he was pressed into these measures by the irresistible importunity of his young warriors. The assurance, on the other hand, of the equity of our ancestors, in giving the natives an equivalent for their lands, is highly consoling. The upright and pious Governor Winslow, in a letter dated at Marshfield, 1st May, 1676, observes: 'I think I can clearly say, that before these present troubles broke out, the English did not possess one foot of land in this colony, but what was fairly obtained by honest purchase of the Indian proprietors. We first made a law, that none should purchase, or receive of gift, any land of the Indians, without the knowledge and allowance of our court. And lest yet they should be streightened, we ordered that Mount Hope, Pocasset, and several other necks of the best land in the colony, because most suitable and convenient for them, should never be bought out of their hands.' See Hubbard's Narrative, (where this important letter is inserted entire,) and Hazard, Coll. ii. 531—534."—*Holmes's American Annals*, vol. I. p. 365.

Whatever wrongs Philip may have sustained during his life, from the arms and pens of his enemies, it seems that his shade will be fully propitiated in the present day. He will have Mr. Southey for his bard; and has already had Mr. Irving for his biographer. To those who have had occasion to examine the rude annals of the earlier settlers in the east, it must surely be a matter of admiration, to see with what facility and grace the author of Knickerbocker has extricated and made use of all the prominent and interesting particulars in the history of that period.

Fiercely they trim their crested hair.

"Then she called for the Mount Hope men, who made a formidable appearance, with their faces painted, and their hair trimmed up in comb-fashion, with their powder-horns and shot-bags at their backs; which among that nation is the posture and figure of preparedness for war." *Thomas Church's "Entertaining History of King Philip's War, &c." Boston,* 1716. *Newport, reprinted,* 1772. By *comb-fashion,* is meant a crest, from the forehead to the back of the head. "The priests in Secota," says Purchas, "haue their haire on the crowne like a combe, the rest being cut from it: only a foretop on their forehead is left, and that combe. They are great wisards." *Purchas' Pilgrim. Part* 3d, p. 949. "Table 2. is an Indian man in his summer dress. The upper part of his hair is cut short, to make a ridge which stands up like the comb of a cock, the rest is either shorn off, or knotted behind his ear." *History of Virginia, Second edition, London,* 1722; said in a manuscript note, in the copy belonging to the New-York Historical Library, to be by one Robert Beverly.

Their peag bells.

The author last mentioned calls the wampum beads *peak;* it is generally written peag. "The women of distinction," says he, "wear deep necklaces, pendants and bracelets, made of small cylinders of the Conque shell, which they call peak." The white beads were made from the hollow of conchs; the purple, which were most prized, from muscle shells. They were strung on leather. *Colden's History of the Five Nations, Hickewelder, &c.* And see a subsequent note to this Canto.

Stanza V.

The red fire is blazing.

"It being now about sun-setting, or near the dusk of the evening, the Netops came running from all quarters loaden with the tops of dry pines, and the like combustible matter, making a huge pile thereof, near Mr. Church's shelter, on the open side thereof; but by this time supper was brought in, &c. but by the time supper was over, the mighty pile of pine knots and tops, &c. was fired, and all the Indians, great and small, gathered in a ring round it. *Awashonks*, with the oldest of her people, men and women mixed, kneeling down made the first ring next the fire, and all the lusty stout men standing up made the next, and then all the rabble in a confused crew surrounded on the out side. Then the chief Captain stepped in between the rings and the fire, with a spear in one hand, and a hatchet in the other, danced round the fire, and began to fight with it, making mention of all the several nations and companies of Indians in the country that were enemies to the English; and at naming of every tribe, he would draw out and fight a new fire-brand, and at finishing his fight with each particular fire-brand, would bow to him and thank him; and when he had named all the several nations and tribes, he stuck down his spear and hatchet, and came out, and another stept in and acted over the same dance, with more fury, if possible, than the first; and when about half a dozen of their chiefs had thus acted their parts, the captain of the guard stept up to Mr. Church and told him, "*They were making soldiers for him*," &c. *Church's History*, p. 49, 50.

The hills of Pocasset replied to the call,
And their Queen, &c.

Weetamoe, the sunk* squaw, or Squaw Sachem of the Pocassets, was a kinswoman of Philip. Captain Church was hard beset by her people, at the breaking out of the war. She is not to be con-

* *Written* Snuke *in the very incorrect modern edition of Hubbard.*

founded with Awashonks, Squaw Sachem of the Seaconets, who dwelt southerly from the Pocasset Indians.

STANZA VI.

Thro' Narraganset's countless clan.

"East of Connecticut were the Narraganset Indians: these were a numerous and powerful body. When the English settled Plymouth, their fighting men were reckoned at three or four thousand; fifty years after this time they were estimated at two thousand. The Pequots and Narragansets maintained perpetual war, and kept up an implacable animosity between them." *Trumbull,* I. 43. This jealousy was a great source of safety to the English, both in the Pequot war, when they were joined by the Narragansets, and in the war with Philip, when the Pequods (or Mohegans) assisted them in exterminating the Narragansets. The Niantics or Nehantics, were a branch of the Narragansets, who joined the English interest, under their Sachem Aganemo. For a further account of the Narragansets see *Gookin.*

The tributary Nipnets heard.

"On the northeasterly and northern part of the colony, were the Nipmuck Indians. Their principal seat was about the great ponds in Oxford, in Massachusetts, but their territory extended southward into Connecticut, more than twenty miles."—*Trumbull,* I. 43. These people are also called Nipnets by Hubbard; it has been already mentioned, that they were tributary to the Pawkanawkutts. The situation of all these tribes is thus briefly given by Hubbard. "The sea-coast, from the pitch of Cape Cod, to the mouth of Connecticut river, [was,] inhabited by several nations of Indians, Wampanoogs, (the first authors of the present rebellion,) Narragansetts, Pequods, Mohegins, as the more inland part of the country by the Nipnets (a general name for all inland Indians betwixt the Massachusetts and Connecticut river.")

STANZA VII.

But Sausaman untimely slain.

Sausaman was the son of Christian Indians, but apostatized, and became King Philip's secretary, who, as Dr. Mather sarcastically remarks, could not even read. A letter dictated by Philip, and written by Sausaman, is preserved in the collections of the Massachusetts Historical Society, vol. II. p. 40. Sausaman afterwards returned to the English, and became an instructor among the Indians. In the year 1674, he informed the Governor of Plymouth, that Philip was plotting with all the Indian nations, to destroy the English. Little notice was taken of this communication at first. But Sausaman was, soon after, found murdered on Assawamsett pond, at a place now called Middleborough, Massachusetts. When he was missed, the neighbours sought for and found the dead body, which had been put under a hole in the ice; but his hat and gun, being left, led to the discovery. " A jury was impanelled," says C. Mather, " and it was remarkable, that one *Tobias*, a Counsellor of King ***Philip's***, whom they suspected as the author of this murder, approaching to the *dead body*, it would still *fall a bleeding afresh*, as if it had been newly slain, &c. Afterwards an Indian, called *Patuckson*, gave in his testimony, that he saw this *Tobias*, with certain other Indians, killing of *John Sausaman*, &c. Hereupon Tobias, with two other Indians, being apprehended, they were, after a fair trial, by a *jury* consisting half of English, and half of Indians, convicted, and so condemned; and though they were all successively turned off the ladder at the gallows, utterly denying the fact, yet the last of them happening to break or slip the rope, did, before his going off the ladder again, confess that the other Indians did really murder John Sausaman, and that he was himself, though no actor in it, yet a looker on. Things began by this time to have an *ominous* aspect."—*Math. Magnalia*, VII. 46. a. See also *Hubbard*, new edit. 66—71. *Church*, 9. *Increase Mather*, 2. and the *Postscript* to the same; also the *Postscript* in the old edition of *Hubbard*, apologizing for the justness of the war, &c.

" *Philip*, conscious to his own guilt, pusht on the execution of his *plot* as fast as he could; he armed his *men*, and sent away their *women*, [to the Narragansets,] and entertained many strange Indians that flocked in unto him from several parts of the country, and began to be tumultuous."—*C. Mather ubi supra.*

Thus broke out King Philip's war, which terminated in almost the total extermination of his allies. Happily for the settlers, it commenced prematurely. The Sachem's plans were general, and deeply laid. The Narragansets had promised to rise with four thousand men, according to Hubbard. It is unnecessary to make any particular references on the miseries of war, alluded to in Stanza VII.

STANZA VIII.

Till Narraganset's fortress blazed.

In the winter of 1675–6, the Commissioners of the United Colonies determined to attack the Narraganset fortress, situated near Pawcatuck river, "on an elevated ground, or piece of upland, of perhaps 3 or 4 acres, in the middle of a hedious swamp; about seven miles nearly due west from *Narraganset* south ferry."—*Church*, 29. The following account of that tragical business is the most full and perspicuous.

"The next morning, (Dec. 19th,) at the dawning of the day, they commenced their march towards the enemy, who were in a swamp at about fifteen miles distance. The troops proceeded with great spirit, wading through the snow, in a severe season, until nearly one o'clock, without fire to warm or food to refresh them, except what had been taken on the way. At this time, they had arrived just upon the seat of the enemy. This was upon a rising ground, in the centre of a large swamp. It was fortified with palisades, and compassed with a hedge without, nearly of a rod's thickness. The only entrance which appeared practicable, was over a log, or tree, which lay up five or six feet from the ground. This opening was commanded in front by a kind of log house, and on the left by a flanker. As soon as the troops entered the skirts of the swamp, they discovered an advanced party of the enemy, upon whom they immediately fired. The enemy returned the fire, and retired before them, until they were led to the very entrance by the blockhouse. Without reconnoitering the fort, or waiting for the army to march up and form for the attack, the Massachusetts troops, led on by their officers, with great courage, mounted the tree and entered the fort: but they were so galled from the blockhouse, and received such a furious and well-directed fire from almost every quarter, that, after every exertion of skill and courage, of which they were capable, they were obliged to retreat out of the fort. The whole army pressed forward with the utmost courage and exertion, but such were the obstructions from the swamp and the snow, that it was a considerable time before the men could all be brought up to action. Captains Johnson and Davenport, and many brave men of the Massachusetts, were killed. The Connecticut troops, who formed in the rear, coming up to the charge, mounted over the log before the blockhouse, the Captains leading and spiriting up the men in the most undaunted manner. About the same time that the main body of the Connecticut troops were forcing their way by the blockhouse, a few bold men ran round to the opposite part of the fort, where they found a narrow spot where there were no palisades, but a high and thick hedge of trees and brush. The sharpness of the action in the front had drawn off the enemy from this part, and climbing over unobserved, they ran down between the wigwams, and poured a heavy and well-directed fire upon the backs of the enemy, who lay wholly exposed to their shot. Thus assaulted, in front and rear, they were driven from the flanker and blockhouse. The Captains crying out, they run, they run, the men pressed so furiously upon them, that they were forced from that part of the fort. The soldiers without rushed in, with great spirit, and the enemy were driven from one covert and hiding place to another, until the middle of the fort was gained; and after a long and bloody action, they were totally routed and fled into the wilderness. As they retired, the soldiers set fire to the wigwams, about six hundred of which were instantly consumed. The enemy's corn, stores, and utensils, with many of their old men, women, and children, perished in the conflagration. It was supposed, that three hundred warriors were slain, besides many wounded, who afterwards died of their wounds and with the cold. Nearly the same number were taken, with three hundred women and children. From the number of wigwams in the fort, it is probable that the whole number of the Indians was nearly four thousand. Those who were not killed in battle, or did not perish in the flames, fled to a cedar swamp, where they spent the night, without food, fire, or covering. It was, nevertheless, a dearly bought victory. Six brave Captains fell in the action, and eighty men were killed or mortally wounded. A hundred and fifty were wounded, who afterwards recovered. After the fatiguing march, and hard fought battle of three hours, in which the troops had been exercised, the army, just at the setting of the sun, having burnt and destroyed all in their power, left the enemy's ground, and, carrying about two hundred dead and wounded men, marched back, sixteen or eighteen miles, to head quarters. The night was very cold and stormy. The snow fell deep, and it was not until midnight, or after, that the army got in. Many of the wounded, who otherwise might have recovered, died with the cold," &c.—*Trumbull's History of Connecticut, Vol. I. pp.* 338—340. See also *Mather's Magnalia*, 49, 50. *Hubbard*, 130—133. *Increase Mather*, 20. Captain Church was severely wounded in this action. "He was struck with three bullets, one on his thigh, which was near half cut off as it glanced on the joint of his hip bone; another through the gatherings of his breeches and drawers, with a small flesh wound; a third pierced his pockets, and wounded a pair of mittens, that he had borrowed of Captain *Prentice;* being wrapped up together had the misfortune of having many holes cut through them with one bullet; however, he made shift to keep on his legs," &c.—*Church*, 27. This kind of defensive armour seems to have been not unusual in those chivalrous days. "Mr. Gill was struck with a musket ball on the side of his belly; but being clad with a buff coat, and some thickness of paper under it, it never broke his skin."—*Church*, 11.

STANZAS IX. and X.

Till of the tribes whom rage at first, &c.

The jealousies of the confederated Indians, among themselves, hastened their separation, and consequent destruction in detail. "This quarrel proceeded to that height, that from that time forward, those several Indians that had for so long a time been combined together, resolved now to part, and every one to shift for themselves, and return to their own homes; Philip to Mount Hope, and the Narragansetts to their own country again; the Nipnets and the River [Connecticut] Indians bending their course westward, others northward," &c.—*Hubbard*, 211. C. Mather says their demons deserted them. See Notes to Canto III.

Of the once powerful nation of the Narragansets, Mr. Hubbard, immediately after the war, says, "there is none of them left on that side of the country, unless some few, not exceeding seventy in number, that have sheltered themselves under the inhabitants of Rhode-Island, as a merchant of that place, worthy of credit, lately affirmed to the writer hereof. It is considered by what degrees they have been consumed and destroyed."—*Hubbard, New Ed.* p. 158. Most of the persecuted tribes went westward, and were never heard of thereafter. Some settled among Moheagans, on the Hudson river. An incredible number were executed at different places.

Those who in slavery's galling chain, &c.

"After this," says Church, "Dartmouth's distresses required succour, great part of the town being laid desolate, and many of the inhabitants killed; the most of Plymouth forces were ordered thither; and coming to Russel's garrison at Ponoganset, they met with a number of the enemy that had surrendered themselves prisoners on terms promised by Captain *Eels* of the garrison, and Ralph Earl, who persuaded them (by a friend Indian he had employed) to come in. And had their promises to the Indians been kept, and the Indians fairly treated, it is probable that most, if not all the Indians in those forts had soon followed the example of the Indians who had now surrendered themselves; which would have been a good step towards finishing the war. But in spite of all that Captains Eels, *Church*, or *Earl*, could say, argue, plead, or beg, somebody else that had more power in their hands, improved it; and without any regard to the promises made them on their surrendering themselves, they were carried away to *Plymouth, there sold, and transported out of the country, being about eight score persons.*"

In another place, the narrator says, "They met the General, and presented him with 18 of the enemy they had captived. The General, pleased with the exploit, gave them thanks, particularly to Mr. *Church,* the mover and chief actor of the business, and sending two of them (likely boys) a *present* to *Boston;* smiling at Mr. *Church* told him, *that he made no doubt his faculty would supply them with* Indian boys *enough before the war was ended.*"

Again; "Captain *Church* hastening with his prisoners through the woods to *Plymouth,* disposed of them all, except only one *Jeffery,* who proved very ingenuous and faithful to him, in informing him where other parcels of Indians harboured," &c. E.

STANZA XI.

When all whom kin or friendship made
To his fallen fortunes dear, were dead.

Philip's uncle *Uncompoën*, sometimes called *Uncomdaen*,* was slain July 31st, 1676, and his sister taken prisoner, at the same time. On the second of August, he narrowly escaped from Captain Church, leaving his peag, wife and son. His friends of any distinction among the other tribes, had been killed before, viz: Canonchet, Pomham, Matoonas, &c.

And bullets whispered death was near.

Among Philip's other hairbreadth deliverances, the following is recorded by Captain Church; it happened on Taunton river, near Bridgewater. "Next morning Captain Church moved very early with his company, which was increased by many of Bridgewater, that enlisted under him for that expedition, and by their piloting, soon came very still to the top of the great tree which the enemy had fallen across the river; and the captain spy'd an Indian sitting on the stump of it on the other side of the river, and he clapp'd his gun up, and had doubtless dispatched him, but that one of his own Indians called hastily to him not to fire, for he believed it was one of their own men; upon which the Indian upon the stump look'd about, and Captain Church's Indian seeing his face, perceived his mistake, for he knew him to be Philip, clapp'd up his gun and fired, but it was too late, for Philip immediately threw himself off the stump, leap'd down a bank on the side of the river, and made his escape."—*Church*, 62.

STANZA XII.

South from the tangled swamp that spread
Below the mount, an upland rose.

"*Philip* was now upon a little spot of upland, that was in the south end of the miry swamp, just at the foot of the mount, which was a spot of ground that *Captain Church* was well acquainted with."—*Idem*, 70.

So spreads beneath the liquid surge.

"The Indians," says C. Mather, "covered themselves with green

* *Akkompoin*, according to Church.

boughs, a subtilty of the same *nature*, though not of the same *colour*, that they affirm to be used by the Cuttle fish."

Stanza XIII.

The Paniese.

"The Counsellors of the Indian kings in New-England were termed the Paniese. These were not only the wisest, but largest and bravest men to be found among their subjects. They were the immediate guard of their respective Sachems, who made neither war nor peace, nor attempted any weighty affair, without their advice." "These paniese, or ministers of state, were in league with the priests, or powaws. To keep the people in awe, they pretended, as well as the priests, to have converse with the invisible world, and that Hobbamock* often appeared to them."—*Trumbull.*

Stanza XIV.

When in his royalties he sate.

"The moon now shining bright, he saw him [Annawon] at a distance coming with something in his hands, and coming up to Captain Church, he fell upon his knees before him, and offered him what he had brought, and speaking in plain English, said, *Great Captain, you have killed Philip, and conquered his country; for I believe that I and my company are the last that war against the English, so suppose the war is ended by your means; and therefore these things belong unto you.* Then opening his pack, he pulled out Philip's belt curiously wrought with wompom, being nine inches broad, wrought with black and white wompom, in various figures and flowers, and pictures of many birds and beasts. This, when hung upon Captain Church's shoulders, reached his ancles; and another belt of wompom he presented him with, wrought after the former manner, which Philip was wont to put upon his head; it had two flags on the back part, which hung down on his back; and another small belt with a star upon the end of it, which he used to hang on his breast; and they were all edged with red hair, which Annawon said they got in the Mohog's country. Then he pulled out two horns of glazed powder, and a red cloth blanket.

---

* Supposed by the English to be the devil. See Notes to Canto IV.

He told Captain Church these were Philip's royalties, which he was wont to adorn himself with when he sat in state."—*Church*, p. 84. I have seen a cape, made of feathers, said to have been Philip's, and a pouch of the same materials, at Brown College, in Providence. The Antiquarian Society in Rhode-Island profess, I believe, to have his skull.

STANZA XV.

As the panther's sight.

I am well aware, that there is, properly, no such American animal; but it is a better sounding word, in poetry, than Cat of the Mountain, &c. I have also called a Couguar a *Tiger*, in the Sixth Canto, to avoid a repetition of the word.

The crystal wave
Where the Spirit dwells in his northern cave.

"About thirty miles below the falls of St. Anthony, at which I arrived the tenth day after I left Lake Pepin, is a remarkable cave of an amazing depth. The Indians term it Wakon-teebe, that is, the Dwelling of the Great Spirit. The entrance into it is about ten feet wide, the height of it five feet. The arch within it is near fifteen feet high and about thirty feet broad. The bottom of it consists of fine clear sand. About twenty feet from the entrance begins a lake, the water of which is transparent, and extends to an unsearchable distance; for the darkness of the cave prevents all attempts to acquire a knowledge of it. I threw a small pebble towards the interior parts of it with my utmost strength: I could hear that it fell into the water, and notwithstanding it was of so small a size, it caused an astonishing and horrible noise, that reverberated through all those gloomy regions. I found in this cave many Indian hieroglyphics, which appeared very ancient, for time had nearly covered them with moss, so that it was with difficulty I could trace them. They were cut in a rude manner, upon the inside of the walls, which were composed of a stone so extremely soft that it might easily be penetrated with a knife; a stone every where to be found near the Mississippi. The cave is only accessible by ascending a narrow steep passage, that lies near the brink of the river."—*Carver's Travels*, pp. 39, 40.

Stanza XIX.

Yet does our warm breath buoyant rise, &c.

"Whither is that breath flown, which a few hours ago sent up smoke to the Great Spirit?"—*Carver's Travels*, p. 262. The usual Indian metaphors for war and peace, are generally known.—"Straight roads, smooth waters, clear sky, smoking the white calumet on a beaver blanket, under the tree of peace, the war kettle, &c. &c." are terms familiar to all who have looked into Colden's History of the Five Nations, Carver's Travels, &c.—I have not, therefore, thought it needful to make any note on particular expressions of this description. The following list of metaphors is extracted from Heckewelder, and comprises, I believe, most of those employed in the text.

"'The sky is overcast with dark blustering clouds.' We shall have troublesome times; we shall have war.—'A black cloud has arisen yonder.' War is threatened from that quarter, or from that nation.—'The path is already shut up.' Hostilities have commenced. The war is begun.—'The rivers run with blood.' War rages in the country.—'To bury the hatchet.' To make, or conclude a peace.—'To lay down the hatchet, or to slip the hatchet under the bedstead.' To cease fighting for a while, during a truce; or, to place the hatchet at hand, so that it may be taken up again at a moment's warning.—'The hatchet you gave me was very sharp.' As you have satisfied me, I have done the same for you; I have killed many of your enemies.—'Singing birds.' Tale bearers—story tellers—liars.—'Don't listen to the singing of the birds which fly by.' Don't believe what stragglers tell you.—'To kindle a council fire at such a place.' To appoint a place where the national business is to be transacted; to establish the seat of government there.—'I will place you under my wings.' (Meaning under my arm pits.) I will protect you at all hazards. You shall be perfectly safe; nobody shall molest you.—'Suffer no grass to grow on the war path.' Carry on the war with vigour.—'To open a path from one nation to another, by removing the logs, brush and briers out of the way.' To invite the nation to which the path leads, to a friendly intercourse; to prepare the way to live on friendly terms with them.—'I have covered yon spot with fresh earth; I have raked leaves, and planted trees thereon;' means literally, I have hidden the grave from your eyes; and figuratively, 'you must now be cheerful again!'—'To bury deep in the earth.' (An injury done.)—To consign it to oblivion."—*Heckewelder*, pp. 125, 126, 127, 128, 129.

As the wretch by subtle sorcerer near.

"It is incredible to what a degree the superstitious belief in witchcraft operates on the mind of an Indian. The moment his imagination is struck with the idea he is bewitched, he is no longer himself. Of this extraordinary power of their conjurers, of the causes which produce it and the manner in which it is acquired, they have not a very definite idea. The sorcerer, they think, makes use of some deadening substance, which he conveys to the person he means to 'strike,' in a manner which they can neither understand nor describe. The person thus 'stricken,' is immediately seized with an unaccountable terror. His spirits sink, his appetite fails, he is disturbed in his sleep, he pines and wastes away, or a fit of sickness seizes him, and he dies at last, a miserable victim to the workings of his own imagination."—*Heckewelder*, 229—231. See also *Carver, Charlevoix, Bartram, Hearne, &c. referred to in Dr. Jarvis's Discourse on the Religion of the Indian tribes, &c. delivered before the N. Y. Historical Society, December* 20, 1819. And see Notes to Canto IV. Dr. Jarvis, p. 51, takes notice of the mistake, made by Carver and others, in confounding the Jongleurs, or Jugglers, (in English,) with the Priests. The expression, *Sorcerer*, made use of in the text, alludes to the former order. I have generally, however, termed them *Pow-wahs*, and their brethren, who followed the more regular practice, *Prophets*. It is somewhat singular that Mr. Southey, in one of his 'Songs of the North-American Indians,' should put the French term *Jongleur*, in the mouth of a native.

Like the coward ghosts whom the bark of stone.

"They believe, (the Chepewyans,) that immediately after their death, they pass into another world, where they arrive at a large river, on which they embark in a stone canoe, and that a gentle current bears them on to an extensive lake, in the centre of which is a most beautiful island; and that, in the view of this delightful abode, they receive that judgment for their conduct during life, which terminates their final state and unalterable allotment. If their good actions are declared to predominate, they are landed upon the island, where there is to be no end to their happiness; which, however, according to their notions, consists in an eternal enjoyment of sensual pleasure, and carnal gratification. But if their bad actions weigh down the balance, the stone canoe sinks at once, and leaves them up to their chins in the water, to behold and regret the reward enjoyed by the good, and eternally struggling, but with unavailing endeavours, to reach the blissful island, from which they are excluded for ever."—*Mackenzie's Voyages*, p. 84, *New-York Ed.* 1802.

The hunters came, the charm they brought.

It is said in Bartram's travels, that the deer are enticed by the olive leaves.

STANZA XXI.

Taubut. "Thank you."—*Heckewelder.*

As fierce the enclosing circle burns.

"Les Chasseurs se rangent sur quatre Lignes, qui forment un très grand Quarré, et commencent par mettre le feu aux Herbes, qui sont séches alors, et fort hautes; puis, à mesure que le feu gagne, ils avancent en se reserrant. Les Bœufs, qui craignent extrêmement le feu, fuyent toujours, et se trouvent à la fin si serrés les uns contre les autres, qu'on les tuë ordinairement jusqu'au dernier." "Quand il [le bœuf] est blessé, il est furieux, et se retourne sur les chasseurs."—*Charlevoix, Tom.* III. 131.

STANZA XXIII.

Miantonimo's honoured head.

I know not if the quantity of this word be correct. Miantonimo was the chief Sachem of the Narragansets, and was defeated and taken prisoner, in a pitched battle with Uncas, who cut off his head and sent it to the English. They stuck it on a pole, *in terrorum*, Anno 1643. Canonchet was Miantonimo's son. He was captured in 1676 by the Connecticut forces, and their Indian confederates, the Mohegans, and Niantics, under their Sachem, old Ninigret. Canonchet was one of the most gallant chieftains of that day. A very interesting account, too long to be inserted, is given of his capture, in Hubbard, pp. 159—162. He was *honour-*

ably shot by some Mohegans of his own rank. Mr. Irving has mentioned him in his life of Philip. Panoquin was the friend of Canonchet, and also a Sub-Sachem among the Narragansets.—*Hubbard. Mather's Magnalia. Increase Mather, &c.*

Ne'er from his path shall traveller turn,
Beside their grassy mound to mourn.

"But on whatever occasion they [the Indians' mounds] may have been made, they are of considerable notoriety among the Indians: for a party passing, about thirty years ago, through the part of the country where this barrow is, went through the woods directly to it, without any instructions or inquiry; and having staid about it for some time, with expressions which were construed to be those of sorrow, they returned to the high road, which they had left about half a dozen miles to pay this visit, and pursued their journey."—*Jefferson's Notes*, pp. 161, 162.

STANZA XXIV.

The battle-god.

"Il paroît, Madame, que dans ces Chansons on invoque le dieu de la guerre, que les Hurons appellent *Areskoui* et les Iroquois *Agreskoué*. Je ne sçai pas quel nom ou lui donne dans les Langues Algonquines." "*L'Areskoui* des Hurons et *l'Agreskoué* des Iroquois est dans l'opinion de ces peuples le Souverain Etre, et le Dieu de la Guerre."—*Charlevoix*, III. 207—344. I do not know, any better than Father Charlevoix, the name of the war-god among the Lenapé; but find a totally different word for the verb *to make war*, which, in the Iroquois, is derived from the name of the deity. The New-England Indians, I believe, had no such person in their mythology.* The word is, therefore, improperly put in King Philip's mouth. Mr. Campbell writes it *Ariouski*, in "Gertrude of Wyoming."

STANZA XXV.

So where at first with gurgling rush.

"I observed that the main body of the Fox river came from the southwest, that of the Ouisconsin from the northeast. That

* See the Notes to Canto IV.

two such rivers should take their rise so near each other, and after running different courses, empty themselves into the sea, at a distance so amazing, (for the former having passed through several great lakes, and run upwards of two thousand miles, falls into the Gulf of St. Lawrence, and the other, after joining the Mississippi, and having run an equal number of miles, disembogues itself into the Gulf of Mexico,) is an instance scarcely to be met in the extensive continent of North-America. I had an opportunity the year following, of making the same observations on the affinity of various head branches of the waters of the St. Lawrence and the Mississippi [which] in some places approached so near that I could have stepped from the one to the other."—*Carver's Travels*, p. 28.

STANZA XXVI.

Enkindles at polluted fires—
The stem must crack.

"They will not suffer any belonging to them to fetch such things as are necessary, even fire, from these retreats, though the want is attended with the greatest inconvenience. They are also so superstitious as to think, if a pipe stem cracks, which among them is made of wood, that the possessor has lighted it at one of these polluted fires," &c.—*Carver's Travels*, 152. This alludes to a particular custom, to which the simile in the text has no reference. See, also, for that custom, *Adair's History of the North-American Indians. M'Kenzie's History of the Fur Trade*, p. 87. *Star in the West, by Dr. Boudinot*, &c. and the Notes to Canto IV.

STANZA XXVII.

No Weko-lis shall ever sing.

"The Indians say that when the leaf of the white oak, which puts forth in the spring, is of the size of the ear of a mouse, it is time to plant corn; they observe that now the whipperwill has arrived, and is continually hovering over them, calling out his Indian name '*Wekolis*,' in order to remind them of the planting time, '*Hackihack*!' go to planting corn!"—*Heckewelder*, p. 305. Carver, mentioning the same circumstance, says the Indians term the bird "*Muckawiss*."—p. 310.

The blasting wind with poisoned breath.

The mortality among the Indians, previous to the coming of the English, has been mentioned before, in the note from *Gookin*, on the Pawkanawkutts. And see Notes to Canto III.

The Owannox.

This was the name given to the English by the Indians. Thus, when the enemy approached Mystic Fort, the sentry of the Pequods cried out O wanux! O wanux! or, as C. Mather has it, Wannux! Wannux!—*Magnalia*, VII. 42.

The gloomy ghosts of dead renown,

Is, I perceive, borrowed from Young,—

The melancholy ghosts of dead renown,
All point to earth, and hiss at human pride!

STANZA XXVIII.

The council fire.

"*One house, one fire, and one canoe*, is to say that they constituted together one people, one family."—*Heckewelder*, 79.

Mysterious as the wave,
Where Huron disembogues its tides.

I transcribed these lines hastily, without referring to their precise allusion. The second line may be stricken out, without injuring the sense of the passage. Those, however, who are disposed to be captious, are perfectly welcome to all the blunders *I* may have committed, here and elsewhere.

"I had like to have omitted a very extraordinary circumstance, relative to these straights, (Michillimackinack.) According to observation, made by the French, whilst they were in possession of the fort, although there is no diurnal flood or ebb to be perceived in these waters, yet, from an exact attention to their state, a periodical alteration in them has been discovered. It was observed that they rose by gradual, but almost imperceptible degrees, till they had reached the height of about three feet. This was accomplished in seven years and a half; and in the same space they as gently decreased, till they had reached their former situation; so that in fifteen years they had completed this inexplicable revolution."—*Carver*, p. 92.

STANZA XXX.

Go howl around the walls of heaven!

"He," the Prophet, "likewise told me, that departed souls always went southward; and that the difference between the good and bad was this—that the former were admitted into a beautiful town, with spiritual walls, or walls agreeable to the nature of souls; and that the latter would for ever hover round those walls, and in vain attempt to get in," &c.—*Diary of David Brainerd.* E. See also *Carver*, p. 251. *M'Kenzie*, &c. &c.

The white man's arms.

Cotton Mather thus pathetically laments the introduction of fire-arms among the Indians. "After this the Land rested from War for forty Years together, even until the Sins of the Land called for a *new Scourge;* and the *Indians* by being taught the Use of *Guns*, which hitherto they had not learnt, were more capable to be made the Instruments of inflicting it. The English Interest in *America* must at last, with Bleeding Lamentations, cry out *Heu! patior telis vulnera facta meis.* For after this, the *Auri* sacra *Fames*, that *cursed Hunger of Lucre*, in the diverse Nations of Europeans here, in diverse Colonies bordering upon one another, soon furnished the Savages with Tools to destroy those that furnish'd them;—*Tools pregnant with infernal flame*," &c.—*Magnalia*, VII. 44. The Dutch sold great quantities of fire arms to the Indians.

STANZA XXXI.

By Sassacous' honoured bones.

This mode of expression is, I believe, improper for an Indian. The author last quoted has this curious remark, speaking of the destruction of the Pequod Fort. "When they came to see the ashes of their friends mingled with the ashes of the fort, and the Bodies of so many of their Country terribly *Barbikew'd*, where the English had been doing a good morning's work, they Howl'd, they Roar'd, they stamp'd, they tore their hair; and though they did not *Swear*, *(for they knew not how!)* yet they *Curs'd*, and were the Pictures of so many *Devils* in Desperation."—*Magnalia*, VII. 43.

In the fierce Maqua's clime.

The Indians in the western parts of Connecticut, were tributary to the Mohawks. The cry of "a Mohawk! a Mohawk!" struck them with universal panic. The Mohawks announced their coming by the shout, "We are coming, we are coming, to suck your blood!" See *Colden's History*, vol. I. p. 3. and *Trumbull*, p. 56. These conquerors made a descent upon Philip's confederates, during this war, and destroyed numbers of them. See the Notes to Canto III.

STANZA XXXII.

That Philip killed an Indian for proposing terms of peace, and that the brother, or friend, of the deceased, betrayed the Sachem's haunts to the English, are historical facts, recorded by all the contemporary historians of that day. Cotton Mather says, "A man belonging to *Philip* himself, being disgusted at him for killing an Indian, who had propounded an expedient of *peace* with the *English*, ran away from him to *Rhode-Island*, where Captain Church was then recruiting of his weary forces."—*Magnalia*, VII. 45. "One of *Philip's* men (being disgusted at him, for killing an Indian, who had propounded an expedient for peace with the English) ran away from him, and coming to *Road-Island*, informed," &c.—*Increase Mather*, p. 46. "Such had been his inveterate malice and wickedness against the English, that despairing of mercy from them, he could not hear that any thing should be suggested to him about a peace, insomuch as he caused one of his confederates to be killed, for propounding an expedient of peace; which so provoked some of his company, not altogether so desperate as himself, that one of them (being near of kin to him that was killed) fled to Road-Island," &c.—*Hubbard, old edit.* p. 103. See Captain Church's account in a Note to Canto III. As to the mode of Agamoun's execution, it is, I believe, justifiable.

"The Sachem was not only examiner, judge, and executioner, in all criminal cases, but in all matters of justice between one man and another. The Sachem whipped the delinquent, and slit his nose, in cases which required these punishments; and he killed the delinquent, unless he were at a great distance. In this case, in which execution could not be done with his own hands, he sent his knife, by which it was effected. The Indians would not receive any punishment that was not capital, from the hands of any except their Sachems. The Sachems were so absolute in their government, that they contemned the limited authority of the English governors."—*Trumbull*, pp. 52, 53.

"In the time of *Bacon's* rebellion, one of these *Werowances*, [Virginia Sachems] attended by several others of his nation, was treating with the English in *New Kent* county, about a Peace; and during the time of his Speech, one of his Attendants presum'd to interrupt him, which he resented as the most unpardonable Affront that could be offered him, and therefore he instantly took his *Tomahawk* from his girdle, and split the Fellow's head, for his presumption. The poor Fellow dying immediately upon the spot, he commanded some of his men to carry him out, and went on again with his Speech where he left off, as unconcern'd as if nothing had happen'd."—*History of Virginia*, p. 194.

STANZA XXXIV.

The brave, the generous Annawon.

See a Note to Canto V.

As in his dream the Initiate's faith.

See a subsequent Note to this Canto.

Their courage is an old year's flame.

"The Indians esteem the old year's fire, as a most dangerous pollution, regarding only the supposed holy fire, which the Archimagus annually renews for the people."—*Adair*, p. 22.

The insatiate hawk.

"The Cheerake Indians have a pointed proverbial expression, signifying 'The great hawk is at home.'"—*Adair*, p. 17. speaking of the Indian contempt of avarice.

Since childhood's earlier moons were dead, &c.

The following extracts relate to what some writers call "making black boys," and Mr. Heckewelder, "the initiation of boys." See the Notes to Dr. Jarvis's discourse; and to the fourth Canto.

"I do not know how to give a better name (initiation of boys) to a superstitious practice which is very common among the Indians, and, indeed, is universal among those nations that I have become acquainted with. By certain methods which I shall presently describe, they put the mind of a boy in a state of perturbation, so as to excite dreams and visions; by means of which they pretend that the boy receives instructions from certain spirits or unknown agents as to his conduct in life, that he is informed of his future destination and of the wonders he is to perform in his future career throughout the world.

"When a boy is to be thus *initiated*, he is put under an alternate course of physic and fasting, either taking no food whatever, or swallowing the most powerful and nauseous medicines, and occasionally he is made to drink decoctions of an intoxicating nature, until his mind becomes sufficiently bewildered, so that he sees or fancies that he sees visions, and has extraordinary dreams, for which, of course, he has been prepared beforehand. He will fancy himself flying through the air, walking under ground, stepping from one ridge or hill to the other across the valley beneath, fighting and conquering giants and monsters, and defeating whole hosts by his single arm. Then he has interviews with the Mannitto, or with spirits, who inform him of what he was before he was born, and what he will be after his death. His fate in this life is laid entirely open before him, the spirit tells him what is to be his future employment, whether he will be a valiant warrior, a mighty hunter, a doctor, a conjurer, or a prophet. There are even those who learn, or pretend to learn, in this way, the time and manner of their death.

"When a boy has been thus initiated, a name is given to him analogous to the visions that he has seen, and to the destiny that is supposed to be prepared for him. The boy, imagining all that happened to him while under perturbation to have been real, sets out in the world with lofty notions of himself, and animated with courage for the most desperate undertakings. They could always cite numerous instances of valiant men, who, in former times, in consequence of such dreams, had boldly attacked their enemy with nothing but the *Tamahican* in their hand, had not looked about to survey the number of their opponents, but had gone straight forward, striking all down before them."—*Heckewelder*, pp. 238—9.

The extract which follows, is, perhaps, as satisfactory an explanation of this singular custom, as any that has been given since the author's time. The same, or similar rites, being used by the Indians of the north, probably gave occasion to the same superstition among the settlers there, as was entertained by those of the south;

namely, that the savages sacrificed their children to Moloch, or the Devil.

"The Indians have their altars and places of sacrifice. Some say, they now and then sacrifice young children: But they deny it, and assure us, that when they withdraw their children, it is not to sacrifice them, but to consecrate them to the service of their God. *Smith* tells of one of these Sacrifices in his time, from the Testimony of some People, who had been Eye-witnesses. His Words are these." Here follows a quotation from *Smith*, referred to in the Notes to Dr. Jarvis's *Discourse*. He then proceeds; "I take this story of *Smith's* to be only an Example of *Huskanawing*, which being a ceremony then altogether unknown to him, he might easily mistake some of the Circumstances of it.

"The solemnity of *Huskanawing* is commonly practis'd once every fourteen or sixteen years, or oftner, as their young Men happen to grow up. It is an Institution or Discipline which all young Men must pass, before they can be admitted to be of the Number of the great Men, Officers, or *Cockarouses* of the Nation; whereas by Captain *Smith's* Relation, they were only set apart to supply the Priesthood. The whole ceremony of *Huskanawing* is performed after the following manner.

"The choicest and briskest young Men of the Town, and such only as have acquired some Treasure by their Travels and Hunting, are chosen out by the Rulers to be *Huskanawed;* and whoever refuses to undergo this Process, dares not remain among them. Several of those odd preparatory Fopperies are premis'd in the Beginning, which have been before related; but the principal Part of the Business is, to carry them into the Woods, and there keep them under Confinement, and destitute of all Society, for several Months; giving them no other Sustenance, but the Infusion or Decoction of some poisonous, intoxicating Roots; by virtue of which Physick, and by the severity of the Discipline which they undergo, they become stark staring Mad: In which raving Condition they are kept eighteen or twenty Days. During these Extremities, they are shut up, Night and Day, in a strong Inclosure, made on Purpose, one of which I saw, belonging to the *Pamaunkie Indians*, in the Year 1694. It was in Shape like a Sugar-loaf, and every way open like a lattice, for the air to pass through. In this Cage, thirteen young men had been *Huskanaw'd*, and had not been a Month set at liberty when I saw it. Upon this Occasion it is pretended, that these poor Creatures drink so much of that Water of *Lethe*, that they perfectly lose the Remembrance of all former Things, even of their Parents, their Treasure, and their Language. When the Doctors find that they have drank sufficiently of the *Wysoccan*, (so they call this mad Potion,) they gradually restore them to their senses again, by lessening the Intoxication of their Diet; but before they are perfectly well, they bring them back into their Towns, while they are still wild and crazy, through the Violence of the Medicine. After this they are very fearful of discovering any thing of their former Remembrance; for if such a thing should happen to any of them, they must immediately be *Huskanaw'd* again. Thus they unlive their former Lives, and commence Men, by forgetting that they ever have been Boys. The Indians pretend that this violent Method of taking away the Memory, is to release the Youth from all their childish Impressions, and from that strong Partiality to Persons and Things which is contracted before Reason comes to take place." —*History of Virginia*, pp. 175, 176, 177, 178, 179.

This too oft sung the illumined priest.

"One thing," says Dr. Mather, "which emboldened King *Philip* in all his Outrages, was an assurance which his *Magicians*, consulting their *Oracles*, gave him, that no *Englishman should ever kill him*; and indeed if any *Englishman* might have had the Honour of *Killing* him, he must have had a good measure of *Grace* to have repressed the *Vanity of Mind* whereto he would have had some Temptations. But this will not extend the Life of that *Bloody* and *Crafty* Wretch above *half his days!*"—*Magnalia*, vii. p. 54.

Stanza XXXV.

Yamoyden.

A word euphonized by my deceased friend, I believe, from some more uncouth name. All the letters, however, belong to the alphabet of these Indians. The rude sound of the Indian names was distressing to the writers of Philip's age, as appears from several remarks of Mather, and others. The author of some verses, meant to be complimentary, prefixed to Hubbard's Narrative, calls them,

"Names uncouth which near Minshew could reduce,
By's Pollyglotton to the vulgar use."

With all due deference, however, the appellations of many of these chieftains, particularly in the vicinity of Narraganset bay, if connected with classical associations, would seem full as sonorous as the names of the ancient heroes.

Prove if the spirits yet be dumb---
The sacrifice of blood.

See notes to Cantos III. and IV.

NOTES TO CANTO SECOND.

The Virgin Mother's meek full eye.

"Christ himself, and the Virgin Mary had most beautiful eys, as amiable eys as any persons, saith Barradius, that ever lived; but withall so modest, so chaste, that whosoever looked on them, was freed from that passion of burning lust; if we may believe Gerson and Bonaventure, there was no such antidote against it as the Virgin Marie's face."—*Burton's Anat. Mel.*

STANZA III.

Round moon.

So the Indians term the full moon.—*Heckewelder*, p. 307.

STANZA V.

Sad Nora sits.

The name of the heroine was, in the original copy, scriptural. My friend afterwards altered it; and I have left the one he selected.

A Nipnet chieftain wooed and won
Her virgin love.

I believe no example is on record, of a Christian woman, of any refinement, voluntarily leaving her friends, and going off with an Indian. There have been many instances, where they have been carried off by the savages; and, after having become used to their mode of life, refused to return to their connexions. La Hontan and Charlevoix are at issue, on a point respecting the taste of the French women. I quote from a poor translation of the former author, not having the original work. Speaking of the conduct of the savages, at the fair at Montreal, after they have intoxicated themselves a little, he says,—"'Tis a comical sight to see 'em running from shop to shop, stark naked, with their bow and arrow.

The nicer sort of women are wont to hold their fans before their eyes, to prevent their being frighted with the view of their ugly parts. But these merry Companions, who know the brisk She-Merchants as well as we, are not wanting in making an offer, which is sometimes accepted of, when the present is tempting. If we may credit the common report, there are more than one or two of the Ladies of this country, whose Constancy and Vertue have held out against the attacks of several officers, and at the same time vouchsafed a free access to these homely paramours. 'Tis presum'd their Compliance was the effect of Curiosity, rather than of any nice Relish; for, in a word, the Savages are neither brisk nor constant. But whatever is the matter, the women are the more excusable upon this Head, that such opportunities are very unfrequent."—*La Hontan's Voyage to N. America, Done into English, London*, 1703.

" Si par hazard, Madame, vous tombez sur le livre de la Hontan, où il est parlé de cette Foire, donnez vous bien de garde de prendre tout ce qu'il en dit pour des vérités. La vraisemblance n'y est pas même gardée. Les Femmes des Montreal n'ont jamais donné lieu à ce que cet Auteur y met sur leur compte, et il n'y a rien à craindre pour leur honneur de la part des Sauvages. Il est sans exemple qu'aucun d'eux ait jamais pris la moindre liberté avec les Françoises, lors même qu'elles ont été leurs Prisonnieres. Il's n'en sont pas même tentés, et il seroit a souhaiter que les Francois eussent le même dégout des Sauvagesses. La Hontan ne pouvoit pas ignorer ce qui est de notorieté publique en ce Pays ; mais il vouloit égayer ses Mémoires, et pour y réussir, tout lui étoit bon," &c.—*Charlevoix*, III. pp. 142—3.

Stanza VII.

The shores where the wife of the Giant was thrown.

There is a tradition, preserved in the *Collections of the Mass. Hist. Society*, Vol. I. p. 137, of the Indians on one of the Islands near Narraganset bay. They say that a giant, called Moshup, one of their ancestors, getting in a passion with his wife, hurled her through the air, and she dropped on Seaconet point. There she beguiled those who were passing on the water, with a melancholy song, which drew them to the shore, where she made them pay her tribute. She finally turned into stone.

STANZA IX.

The Wakon bird descends from heaven.

"The Wakon bird, as it is termed by the Indians, appears to be of the same species as the birds of paradise. The name they have given it is expressive of its superior excellence and the veneration they have for it; the Wakon bird being in their language the bird of the Great Spirit. It is nearly the size of a swallow, of a brown colour, shaded about the neck with a bright green; the wings are of a darker brown than the body; its tail is composed of four or five feathers, which are three times as long as its body, and which are beautifully shaded with green and purple. It carries this fine length of plumage in the same manner as a peacock does," &c.—*Carver*, p. 814. *Wakon*, however, is the term for God, or the Great Spirit, in the Naudowessie dialect. In the Language of the Algonquins, Chippewyans, &c. which is radically the same with that of the New-England Indians, the name of the Deity, or Good Spirit, is *Kitchi Manitou;* as that of bad Spirits is *Matchi Manitou.* The term used in the text is therefore improper, as is also, (though less objectionable, as it is applied,) the phrase *Wakon cave*, employed in the Fourth Canto.

The Great good Spirit's beloved speech.

According to Adair, the Southern Indians termed the sacred traditions of their forefathers, "the beloved speech."

STANZA XI.

Wept like the roebuck when he flies.

"On dit qu'il [le Chevreuil] jette des larmes, lorsqu'il se voit poussé à bout par les Chasseurs."—*Charlevoix*, III. p. 132.

STANZA XII.

I sought Seaconet's Queen.

Awashonks, the "Sunke Squaw" of Seaconet, shortly before this time, had submitted, with ninety of her warriors, to Major Bradford. Her Indians accompanied the English in their last chace after

Philip. See *Magnalia*, VII. 53. *Hubbard, New Ed.* 213. *Church*, 21, 43, &c.

Hunter genii.

Charlevoix mentions a feast in honour of what may be supposed to be the Hunter Genius. p. 118.

The wily red fox leap,
To snare the sportive birds.

"Les Renards donnent la chasse aux oiseaux de Riviere, d'une maniere fort ingénieuse. Ils s'avancent un peu dans l'Eau, puis se retirent et font cent cabrioles sur le Rivage. Les Canards, les Outards, et d'autres Oiseaux semblables, que ce jeu divertit, s'approchent du Renard; quand il les voit à sa portée, il se tient fort tranquile d'abord, pour ne les point effaroucher, il renmuë seulement sa Queuë, comme pour les attirer de plus près, et ces sots Animaux donnent dans le piége, jusqu'a becquetter cette Queuë. Alors le Renard saute dessus, et manque rarement son coup."—*Charlevoix*, III. p. 133.

Balmy fountains of the west.

"Un officier digne de foi m'a assûré avoir vû une Fontaine, dont l'Eau est comme de l'Huile, et a le goût de Fer. Il m'a ajoûté qu'un peu plus loin, il y en a une autre toute semblable, et que les Sauvages se servent de son Eau, pour appaiser toutes sortes de douleurs."—*Idem.* p. 224.

STANZA XIII.

The wanderer of the lonely place
Waylaid, and tortured to confess.

"They soon captivated the Numponsets, and brought them in, not one escaping. This stroke he [Church] held several weeks, never returning empty handed. When he wanted intelligence of their kennelling places, he would march to some place likely to meet with some travellers or ramblers, and scattering his company, would lie close, and seldom lay above a day or two, at the most, before some of them would fall into his hands, whom he would compel to inform where their company was; and so, by his method of secret and sudden surprises, took great numbers of them prisoners."—*Church.* E.

All the pure waters of thy faith.

The savages, naturally enough, ascribed supernatural effects to the sacrament of Baptism.—See *Charlevoix*, 249.

STANZA XVI.

"The river St. Mary has its source from a vast lake, or marsh, called Ouaquaphenogan, which lies between Flint and Oukmulge rivers, and occupies a space of near three hundred miles in circuit. This vast accumulation of waters, in the wet season, appears as a lake, and contains some large islands, or knolls, of rich high land; one of which the present generation of the Creeks represent to be a most blissful spot of the earth: they say it is inhabited by a peculiar race of Indians, whose women are incomparably beautiful; they also tell you that this terrestrial paradise has been seen by some of their enterprising hunters, when in pursuit of game, who, being lost in inextricable swamps and bogs, and on the point of perishing, were unexpectedly relieved by a company of beautiful women, whom they call daughters of the sun, who kindly gave them such provisions as they had with them, which were chiefly fruit, oranges, dates, &c. and some corn cakes, and then enjoined them to fly for safety to their own country; for that their husbands were fierce men, and cruel to strangers: they further say that these hunters had a view of their settlements, situated on the elevated banks of an island, or promontory, in a beautiful lake; but that in their endeavours to approach it, they were involved in perpetual labyrinths, and, like enchanted land, still as they imagined they had just gained it, it seemed to fly before them, alternately appearing and disappearing. They resolved, at length, to leave the delusive pursuit, and to return; which, after a number of inexpressible difficulties, they effected. When they reported their adventures to their countrymen, their young warriors were inflamed with an irresistible desire to invade, and make a conquest of, so charming a country; but all their attempts hitherto have proved abortive, never having been able again to find that enchanting spot, nor even any road or pathway to it; yet they say that they frequently meet with certain signs of its being inhabited, as the building of canoes, footsteps of men, &c. They tell another story concerning the inhabitants of this sequestered country, which seems probable enough, which is, that they are the posterity of a fugitive remnant of the ancient Yameses, who escaped massacre after a bloody and decisive conflict between them and the Creek nation, (who, it is certain, conquered, and nearly exterminated, that once powerful people,) and here found an asylum, remote and secure from the fury of their proud conquerors."—*Bartram's travels through North and South Carolina, &c. London*, 1792, pp. 25, 26.

STANZA XVII.

And she had heard an Indian tell,
Such sounds foreboded sudden bale.

"As soon as night comes on, these birds will place themselves on the fences, stumps, or stones that lie near some house, and repeat their melancholy notes without any variation till midnight. The Indians, and some of the inhabitants of the back settlements, think if this bird perches upon any house, that it betokens some mishap to the inhabitants of it."—*Carver*, 311.

It was the soul of a love-lorn maid.

The Author of the "*History of Virginia*," before quoted, makes mention, p. 185, of a bird, said to contain the soul of one of their princes, by the Indians. Their ideas of the transmigration of souls, are referred to in the Notes to Canto V.

STANZA XX.

Each stepping where the first had gone.

"They march one man behind the other, treading carefully in each other's steps, so that their number may not be ascertained by the prints of their feet."—*Heckewelder.*

NOTES TO CANTO THIRD.

Bright as the bird whom Indian legends sing, &c.

"The notion which the Chepewyans entertain of the creation, is of a very singular nature. They believe that at the first the globe was one vast and entire ocean, inhabited by no living creature, except a mighty bird, whose eyes were fire, whose glances were lightnings, and the clapping of whose wings was thunder. On his descent to the ocean, and touching it, the earth instantly arose, and remained on the surface of the waters. This omnipotent bird then called forth all the variety of animals from the earth," &c. &c.—*Mackenzie's Voyages*, p. 74. E.

Stanza I.

The garden of the deep.

The island of Rhode-island has always been celebrated for its picturesque beauty, and the salubrity of its climate. Its surface is delightfully varied into hill and dale, wood and field, and unquestionably merits the appellation here bestowed. It was the rendezvous of the English colonists during the wars with Philip. E.

Stanza X.

The plagues which sleep,
In earth's dark bosom buried deep,
As the poor savage deems.

It is mentioned in "*New England's Memorial*," that the Indians supposed the whitemen had the power of burying the small pox under ground, or letting it escape among them. They were severely afflicted with this disease, particularly in the spring of 1634.

Owing to their total want of comfort and cleanliness, few of them could escape, who caught it. "Being very sore," says the *memorial*, "what with cold and other distempers, they die like rotten sheep." Cotton Mather says, it was the plague, which Squanto told his countrymen the English kept in a cellar.

STANZA XII.

How oft the storm their barks delayed.

The difficulties encountered by the first emigrants, in crossing the ocean, and after their arrival, are generally known.—They are faithfully narrated in the *Magnalia, Prince's Chronological History, New-England's Memorial, Purchas's Collections*, &c. and in the modern histories of *Hutchinson, Trumbull*, &c. It would be useless to make any extracts, in these brief notes, unless required by the text.

STANZA XIII.

A meteor fierce their herald came.

"Some of the ancient Indians, that are surviving at the writing hereof, do affirm, that about some two or three years before the first English arrived here, they saw a blazing star, or comet, which was a forerunner of this sad mortality, for soon after it came upon them in extremity. Thus God made way for his people, by removing the heathen," &c.—*N. E. Memorial, Boston printed, Newport reprinted*, 1772. Of this mortality among the Indians, mentioned in the Notes to Canto first, the Memorial says,—"The Lord was disposed much to waste them by a great mortality, together with which were their own civil dissentions, and bloody wars, so as the twentieth person was scarce left alive when these people arrived, there remaining sad spectacles of that mortality in the place where they seated, by many bones and skulls of the dead lying above ground: whereby it appeared that the living of them were not able to bury them." Id. p. 25.

C. Mather, *Magnalia*, I. 7, speaking of this mortality, says, "It is remarkable, that a Frenchman who not long before these transactions, had by a shipwreck been made a Captive among the Indians of this Country, did, as the Survivors reported, just before he dy'd in their Hands, tell these *Tawny Pagans, that God, being angry with them for their wickedness, would not only destroy them all, but also People the place with another Nation, which would not live after their Brutish Manners.* Those Infidels then Blasphemously reply'd, God could not kill them; which Blasphemous mistake was confuted by an horrible and unusual *Plague*, &c." This story is told more at length, in *N. E. Memorial*, pp. 29, 30.

Their Powahs met with purpose fell.

"But before I pass on, let the reader take notice of a very remarkable particular, which was made known to the planters at Plymouth, some short space after their arrival, that the Indians, before they came to the English to make friendship with them, got all the Powahs in the country, who, for three days together, in a horrid and devilish manner, did curse and execrate them with their conjurations; which assembly and service they held in a dark and dismal swamp. Behold how satan laboured to hinder the gospel from coming into *New England.*" *N. E. Memorial*, p. 32.

STANZA XIV.

Gaunt famine came.

That the miseries of this famine are not exaggerated, may be seen by a reference to the authorities.

Crawled forth the myriad insect host.

"It is to be observed, that the spring before this sickness, there was a numerous company of flies, which were like for bigness unto wasps' bumble-bees; they came out of little holes in the ground, and did eat up the green things, and made such a constant yelling noise, as made the woods ring of them, and ready to deafen the hearers; the Indians said that sickness would follow, and so it did very hot in the months of June, July and August, of that summer." *N. E. Memorial*, 99. The account of the sickness is given in the same place.

On sterile soil.—

Oft blazed their roofs with raging flame—
And oft the fierce tornado came.

See the same book, pp. 43, 103, &c.

STANZA XV.

A mortal terror o'er them came.

This circumstance is particularly dwelt upon, by Nathaniel Morton, (Author of the Memorial,) and C. Mather.

STANZA XVI.

When in their agonies they cried,
On Christ.

" After the English of the Massachusetts were returned, the Pequots took their time and opportunity to cut off some of the English at Connecticut, as they passed up and down upon their occasions; and tortured some of them in putting them to death, in a most barbarous manner, and most blasphemously in (the *Pequots'* horrible blasphemy) this their cruelty, bade them call upon their God, or mocked and derided them when they so did."—*N. E. Memorial*, 107.

" Those who fell into their hands alive, were cruelly tortured, after a most barbarous manner, by insulting over their prisoners in a blasphemous wise, when in their dying agonies, under the extremity of their pains, (their flesh being first slashed with knives, and then filled with burning embers,) they called upon God and Christ, with gasping groans, resigning up their souls into their hands; with which words these wretched caitiffs used to mock the English afterwards, when they came within their hearing and view."—*Hubbard*, pp. 23, 24.

O'er daring sin—
Prolific schism.—

Alluding to the differences in religious opinions, which were so unsavoury in the nostrils of those worthy and stubborn sectarians, who had themselves emigrated that they might enjoy the free exercise of their tenets. One Thomas Morton, at an early period, appears to have been particularly and deservedly obnoxious, for his open profanity. See *N. E. Memorial*, pp. 76, 77. *Magnalia*, &c. This man, among the other offences laid to his charge, is said to have sold guns and powder to the natives.

Wo to the worm whate'er it be!

" But God prepared a worm when the morning rose the next day, and it smote the gourd that it withered."—*Jonah*, c. 4. v. 7.

"Verba Doct. *Arrowsmith*, in Orat. Antiweigelianâ. *Faxit Deus Optimus, Maximus, tenacem adeo veritatis hanc Academiam, ut deinceps, in* Angliâ *Lupum, in* Hiberniâ *Bufonem, invenire facilius sit, quàm aut* Socinianum *aut* Arminianum *in* Cantabrigiâ."—*Magnalia*, iv. 139.

STANZA XVII.

On Moloch's streaming pyre.

See the Notes to Canto IV.

Thus saith the Lord.

Josh. c. 10. v. 8.

STANZA XVIII.

That polluted night
That saw the heathen's damning rite.

"The Indians took five or six of the English Prisoners; and, that the Reader may understand, *crimine ab uno*, what it is to be taken by such *Devils Incarnate*, I shall here inform him: They *Stripp'd* these unhappy Prisoners, and caused them to run the *Gantlet*, and Whipped them after a Cruel and Bloody manner; they then threw Hot Ashes upon them, and cutting off Collops of their Flesh, they put *Fire* into their Wounds, and so, with Exquisite, Leisurely, Horrible Torments, *Roasted* them out of the World."—*Magnalia*, vii. 51. b. "But NOW was the time for Deliverance! There was an *Evil Spirit* of *Dissention* strangely sent among the *Indians*, which disposed them to separate from one another: The *Dæmons*, who visibly exhibited themselves among them at their *Powawing* or Conjuring, signified still unto them, that they could now *do no more for them:* the *Maquas*, a Powerful Nation in the West, made a Descent upon them, ranging and raging through the Desart with irresistible Fury; *Fevers* and *Fluxes* became *Epidemical* among them, &c. And an unaccountable Terror at the same time so Dispirited them, that they were like Men under a Fascination." —*Idem*, p. 52. a.

"Whether for the loss of some of their own company in that day's enterprise, (said to be an hundred and twenty,) or whether it was the Devil in whom they trusted, that deceived them, and to whom they made their address the day before, by sundry conjurations of their powaws; or whether it were by any dread that the Almighty sent upon their execrable blasphemies, which it is said they used in torturing some of their poor captives, (bidding Jesus come and deliver them out of their hands from death, if he could,) sure it is that after this day they never prospered in any attempt they made against the English, but were continually scattered and broken, till they were in a manner all consumed."—*Hubbard, new ed.* p. 186.

Then talked they of the sign beheld
By their advancing troop.

A central eclipse of the moon in Capricorn, according to Hubbard, happened on the 26th of June, when some troops from Boston were on their march to Mount Hope. "Some melancholy fancies would not be persuaded but that the eclipse, falling out at that instant of time, was ominous, conceiving also that in the centre of the moon they discerned an unusual black spot, not a little resembling the scalp of an Indian: As others, not long before, imagined they saw the form of an Indian bow, accounting that likewise ominous, (although the mischiefs following were done by guns, and not by bows.) Both the one and the other might rather have thought of what Marcus Crassus, the Roman General, going forth with an army against the Parthians, once wisely replied to a private soldier, that would have dissuaded him from marching that time, because of an eclipse of the moon in Capricorn, that he was more afraid of Sagittarius than of Capricornus, meaning the arrows of the Parthians," &c.—*Hubbard,* p. 74.

Cotton Mather, recording this circumstance, has the same remark with respect to Sagittarius and Capricornus. This is not the only instance in which he condescends to borrow from Hubbard. The latter, speaking of the butchery, in cold blood, of thirty Pequods, says, "they were turned presently into Charon's ferryboat, under the command of Skipper Gallop, who dispatched them a little without the harbor." This sentimental piece of wit is thus copied in the *Magnalia,* VII. p. 44. "They put the men on board a vessel of one Skipper *Gallop,* which proved a *Charon's* ferryboat unto them, for it was found the quickest Way to feed the Fishes with 'em."

Nor this alone portended war.

"Yea, and now we speak of things *Ominous*, we may add, Some time before this, in a Clear, Still, Sunshiny Morning, there were divers persons in *Malden* who heard in the Air, on the South-East of them, a *Great Gun* go off, and presently thereupon the Report of *Small Guns* like Musket Shot, very thick discharging, as if there had been a *Battel*. But that which most of all astonished them was the Flying of *Bullets*, which came Singing over their Heads, and seemed very near to them; after which the sound of *Drums* passing along Westward was very Audible; and on the same day, in *Plymouth* Colony, in several Places, invisible *Troops* of Horses were heard Riding to and fro."—*Magnalia*, VII. p. 46. For a further account of these prodigies, see *Hubbard*, p. 74. and *Increase Mather*, p. 34, who says he had the relation "from serious, faithfull and Judicious hands, even of those who were ear-witnesses of these things."

Of timely rains, &c.

There are several instances related of the interposition of divine providence in behalf of the English, during their conflicts with the Indians. One of the most remarkable is said to have happened at Bridgewater. We borrow the words of Hubbard. "The Indians presently began to fire the town, but it pleased God so to spirit and encourage several of the inhabitants, issuing out of their garrison houses, that they fell upon them with great resolution, and beat them off; at the same instant of time, the Lord of Hosts also fighting for them from Heaven, by sending a storm of thunder and rain very seasonably, which prevented the burning of the houses which were fired." E.

STANZA XX.

Dark, even in youth, the orphan's fate.

The story of Fitzgerald, previous to his emigration, is irrelevant to our subject. I have retained it however, as it formed so considerable a portion of my friend's share of the poem. I have added three long stanzas, narrating the manner in which the daughter was won and carried off by the Indian. The ideas are probably borrowed from the wooing of Othello. How should they not be?

Like eastern birds of Paradise.

"Manucodiatæ, eastern birds of Paradise, that doe live on aire and dew."—*Burton's Anat. Mel.*

Who follows not the torch of hope, &c.

"Who builds not upon hope," says *Sir Philip Sidney,* "shall fear no earthquake of despair."—*Aphorisms.* So *Seneca,* in *Medea,*

Qui nil potest operare, desperet nihil. E.

STANZA XXIV.

When even the brother had embued
His hands amid his brother's blood;
The parent wept no more his son,
In that disastrous strife undone.

Sed postquam tellus scelere est imbuta nefando,
Iustitiam que omnes cupidâ de mente fugârunt,
Perfudere manus fraterno sanguine fratres,
Destitit extinctos natos lugere parentes, &c. &c.

Propertius, Epithal. Pelei et Thetidos.

STANZA XXV.

Naseby's fatal plain.

The decisive battle of Naseby was fought in the year 1645, with nearly equal forces, on the sides both of the king and parliament. The fortune of the day turned against Charles, and he was finally obliged to quit the field, with a loss of about eight hundred men; though the parliament lost above a thousand. E.

STANZA XXVIII.

Perchance too long alone she strayed, &c.

"As fern grows in untild grounds, and all manner of weeds, so do grose humours in an idle body: *ignavum corrumpunt otia corpus.*" "Cozen german to idleness, and a concomitant cause, which goes hand in hand with it, is *nimia solitudo,* too much solitude—which is either coact, enforced, or else voluntary." "Voluntary solitude is that which is familiar with melancholy, and gently brings on, like a Screw, a shooing horn, or some Sphinx, to this irrevocable gulf. Most pleasant it is at first, to such as are melancholy given, to lie in bed whole dayes, and keep their chambers, to walk alone in some solitary grove, betwixt wood and water, by a brook side, to meditate upon some delightsome and pleasant subject which shall affect them most; *amabilis insania,* and *mentis gratissimus error,* &c. &c. *Anat. Mel.*

STANZA XXXIX.

Is it not written, &c.

Deuteronomy, chap vii. ver. 1—4.

STANZA XXX.

Up to the camp two horsemen rode.

In the account of the means by which the intelligence of Philip was conveyed, we have deviated, not materially however, from historical accuracy, in order the better to interweave it with the story. We quote the following from *Church's* history.—"Not seeing or hearing of any of the enemy, they went over the ferry (from *Pocasset*) to Rhode-Island, to refresh themselves. The Captain, with about half a dozen in his company, took horse and rid about eight miles down the island, to Mr. *Sandford's* where he had left his wife; who no sooner saw him but fainted with surprise; and by that time she was a little revived, they spied two horsemen coming a great pace. Captain *Church* told his company that those men (by their riding) came with tidings. When they came up they proved to be Major *Sandford* and Captain *Golding;* who immediately asked Captain *Church, what he would give to hear some news of* PHILIP? *He reply'd, That was what he wanted. They told him, They had rid hard with some hopes of overtaking him, and were now come on purpose to inform him, that there were just now tidings from Mount-Hope; an Indian came down from thence (where* Philip's *camp now was) on to Sand-point, over against* Trip's, *and halloo'd, and made signs to be fetched over, he reported, That he was fled from Philip, who* (said he) *has killed my* BROTHER *just before I came away, for giving some advice there displeased him.* And said, *he was fled for fear of meeting with the same thing his brother had met with;* told them also, *That* Philip *was now in* Mount-Hope *neck.*" E.

STANZA XXXIV.

And how to dust by sorrow borne, &c.

" *Sir,*" (said some of the Indians to Captain Church,) "*you have now made* Philip *ready to die, for you have made him as poor and miserable as he used to make the* English; *for you have now killed or taken all his relations. That they believed he would now soon have his head, and that this bout had almost broke his heart.*" —Church. E.

NOTES TO CANTO FOURTH.

Mid mazes strange the dancers seem to fly,
Wildly the unwearied hunters drive the Bear.

"Ils (les Iroquois et les Hurons) nomment les Pleyades, *les Danseurs* et les *Dansueses.* Ils donnent le nom *d'Ours* aux quatre premieres de ce que nous appellons la grande Ourse; les trois qui composent sa queuë, ou qui sont le train du Chariot de David, sont, selon eux, trois Chasseurs, qui poursuivent l'Ours ; et la petite Etoile, qui accompagne celle du milieu, est la Chaudiere dont le second est chargé Les Sauvages de l'Acadie nommoient tout simplement cette Constellation et la suivante, la grande et la petite Ourse ; mais ne pourroit-on pas juger que quand ils parloient ainsi au sieur Lescarbot, ils ne répétoient que ce qu'ils avoient oüi dire à plusieurs François ?"—*Charlevoix*, iii. 400.

"It has been surprising unto me to find, that they have always called Charles's Wain by the name of *Paukunnawaw*, or *The Bear*, which is the name by which *Europeans* also have distinguished it." —*Magnalia*, iii. 192.

Manitto,

Or *Spirit.* The word is thus written by Heckewelder. By the English authors it is written Manitou, whence Mr. Campbell has it so, in "Gertrude of Wyoming."

"As when the evil Manitou that dries
The Ohio woods," &c.

The mistake may have arisen from the French authors writing it Manitou, which is pronounced Maneetou.

The incantation which I have introduced in this place, is founded on the subsequent passages from Charlevoix; which are, I believe, abundantly sufficient to justify the expressions in the text, unless it be, perhaps, those in the second verse of the third Stanza, where the Spirit is apostrophized as the Muse, or personification of the imagination itself. I have also taken the liberty of ascribing to one Spirit, the congenial attributes of many. If Father Charlevoix has not been deceived, and led too far by his own fancy, surely, the elements of poetry cannot be denied to our Aborigines.

"Before we launch out into the particulars of their worship, it will be proper to remark that the savages give the name of *Genius* or *Spirit* to all that surpasses their understanding, and proceeds from a cause that they cannot trace. Some of their Spirits they take to be Good, and some Bad; of the former sort are the *Spirit of Dreams*, &c. Of the latter sort are *Thunder*, *Hail falling upon their corn*, *a great Storm*," &c.—*La Hontan*, Vol. ii. p. 30. The Manittos of the Lenapé are the same as the *Okkis* of the Iroquois.—*Charlevoix*, p. 345.

When the Indians had dreams, it was indispensable to their quiet, that the vision should be immediately accomplished. One of them, who dreamed that he was tormented by his enemies, had himself tied to a stake, and would not be pacified, until he had been severely mangled. Many stories of this kind are told by Charlevoix, p. 354. The longest and most curious is that of a Huron woman, narrated p. 230, in the third volume. It is too long to be here inserted; though several ideas in the text are taken from it.

STANZA I. Ver. 2.

Thy whisper creeps where leaves are stirred, &c.

"Et l'on prétend que la présence de l'Esprit se manifeste par un Vent impétueux, qui se leve tout à coup; ou par un Mugissement, que l'on entend sous terre, &c." Charlevoix is here speaking, however, of the Spirit which occasions mental wandering in sickness; which I have identified with the Spirit of Dreams.

STANZA II. Ver. 1.

From the land, &c.

"They (four savages from the west) farther informed us, That the Nation of the *Asseni poulaes*, whose lake is down in the map, and who lie North-East of the *Issatti*, was not above six or seven Days Journey from us: That none of the Nations within their Knowledge, who lie to the West and North-West of them, had any great Lake about their Countries, which were very large, but only Rivers, which coming from the North, run cross the Countries of their Neighbouring Nations, which border on their Confines, on the side of the Great Lake, which in the Language of the Savages is the same as sea. That Spirits, and Pigmies, or men of little Stature, did inhabit them, as they had been informed by People that lived farther up than themselves; and that all the nations which lie beyond their Country, and those which are next to them, do dwell in Meadows and large Fields, where are many wild Bulls and Castors, which are greyer than those of the North, and have their Coat more inclining to Black; with many other wild Beasts, which yield very fine Furrs."—*Hennepin's New Discovery of a Vast Country in America, &c. London, translated, with additions,* 1699.

It is probable that Father Hennepin confounded the general name of the sea, among the savages, with the particular name given to the Assinapoil lake. Charlevoix says, "Le veritable Pays des Assinaboils est aux environs d'un Lac, qui porte leur nom, et que l'on connoit peu. Un François, que j'ai vu à Montreal m'a assûré y avoir été, mais il l'avoit vû, comme on voit la mer dans un Port, et en passant, L'opinion commune est que ce Lac a six cent lieues de circuit; qu'on ne peut y aller que par des chemins presque impratiquables; que tous les Bords en sont charmans, &c. Quelques Sauvages le nomment Michinipi, qui veut dire la *Grande Eau*. C'est bien dommage que ce Lac n'ait pas été connû des Sçavans, qui ont cherché partout le Paradis Terrestre; il auroit été pour le moins aussi bien placé là que dans la Scandinavie." iii. pp. 185.

Ver. 2.

Then to the Chief who has fasted long, &c.

"Celui qui doit commander ne songe point à lever des Soldats qu'il n'ait jeûné plusieurs jours, pendant lesquels il est barbouillé de noir, n'á presque point de conversation avec personne, invoque jour et nuit son Esprit tutelaire, observe surtout avec soin des Songes. La persuasion où il est, suivant le génie présomptueux de ces Barbares, qu'il va marcher à une Victoire certaine, ne manque guéres de lui causer des Rêves selon ses desirs."—*Charlevoix*, iii. pp. 216.

Ver. 3.

Then shall the hunter who waits for thee.

"C'est toujours un Chef de Guerre, qui marque le tems de la chasse de l'ours, et qui a soin d'inviter les chasseurs. Cette invitation est suivie d'une Jeûne de huit jours, pendant lesquels il n'est pas même permis de boire une goutte d'eau. Le Jeûne s'obverve pour obtenir des Esprits qu'ils fassent connôitre où l'on trouvera beaucoup d'ours." &c. &c.—*Charlevoix*, p. 115.

Where the hermit bear
Keeps his long fast.

"Le tems de la chasse de l'Ours est l'Hyver. Alors ces Animaux sont cachés dans les creux d'arbres ; ou s'ils en trouvent d'abattus, ils se font de leurs Racines une Taniere, dont ils bouchent l'entrée, avec des Branches de Sapin, et où ils sont parfaitément à l'abri des rigueurs le da Saison. Si tout cela leur manque, ils font un Trou en Terre, et ont grand soin, quand ils y sont entrés, d'en bien fermer l'ouverture. On est bien assûré qu'il n'y porte ancune provision, et par conséquent que pendant tout ce temps-là il ne boit, ni ne mange."—*Charlevoix*, 117.

With regard to the state in which the savages supposed the soul to be during sleep, Charlevoix has this passage. "Il n'y a rien, sur quoi ces Barbares ayent porté plus loin la superstition, et l'extravagance, que ce qui regarde les Songes ; mais ils varient beaucoup dans la maniere, dont ils expliquent leurs peusées sur cela. Tantôt c'est l'Ame raisonnable, qui se promene, tandis que l'Ame sensitive continue d'animer le corps. Tantôt c'est le Génie familier, qui donne des avis salutaires sur ce qui doit arriver: tantôt c'est une visite, qu'on reçoit de l'Ame de l'Objet, auquel on rêve; mais de quelque façon, que l'on conçoive le Songe, il est toujours regardé comme une chose sacrée, et comme le moyen le plus ordinaire, dont les Dieux se servent pour faire connôitre aux Hommes leurs volontés."—*Charlevoix*, 354.

STANZA III. Ver. 1.

Thine the riddle, strange and dark.

It formed, according to our author, a great amusement of the savages, to tell their dreams in an ænigmatic manner, and compel each other to divine them. A feast of dreams, as it was ordinarily called, but which was named by the Iroquois "the confusion of brains," was occasionally held. Its orgies were fantastical, and sometimes dangerous; for if any one took it into his head to say, that he had dreamed of killing another, the person threatened had need of ready wit, to avert the literal fulfilment of the vision. An account of this festival is given in *Charlevoix*, p. 356. There was another strange custom growing out of this superstition. Previous to entering the enemies' country, the warriors ran about their camp, proclaiming their obscure visions; and he, whose riddle was not satisfactorily guessed, had the privilege of returning without comment or dishonour. "Voila," says *Charlevoix*, "qui donne beau jeu aux Poltrons." p. 237. These ænigmas, as this author repeatedly remarks, were always ascribed to the inspiration of a genius.

Thine to yield the power to mark, &c.

"Il n'est pas étonnant après cela que les Sauvages croyent aux Revenans: aussi en font-ils des contes de toutes les façons. J'ai vû un pauvre Homme, qui à force d'en entendre parler, s'étoit imaginé qu'il avoit toujours une troupe de Morts a ses trousses, et comme on avoit pris plaisir à augmenter sa frayeur, il en etoit devenu fou." p. 374.

Ver. 3.

When of thought and strength despoiled, &c.

"On ne refuse rien au malade de ce qu'il demande, parce que, dit-on, ses desirs en cet état sont des ordres du Génie, qui veille à sa conservation; et quand on appelle les Jongleurs, c'est moins à cause de leur habilité, que parce qu' on suppose, qu'ils peuvent mieux sçavoir des Esprits la cause du mal, et les remedes, qu'il y faut appliquer." "Selon les Iroquois, toute Maladie est un desir de l'Ame, et on ne meurt, que parce que le désir n'est pas accompli." pp. 367. 370.

In consequence of this superstition, they would not begrudge any trouble or danger, to satisfy the wildest wishes of an invalid. The jugglers or quack doctors among them, take advantage of this belief, to prescribe, in desperate cases, the accomplishment of some impossible task, which they pretend is wished by the patient, as the Spirits have revealed to them.—*Id.* p. 368.

Ver. 4.

When the dizzy senses spin, &c.

Fools and madmen were supposed to be entirely under the influence of Spirits. The words of the latter were regarded as oracles.—*Idem.*

Like the Powah, when first within,
The present Spirit feeling.

"Il se commence (le Jongleur) par se faire suer, et quand il est bien fatigué à crier, à se debattre, et à invoquer son Génie, &c. Alors, plein de sa prétenduë Divinité, et plus semblable à un Energumene, qu'a un homme inspiré du Ciel," &c.—*Idem.*

"The Conjurer is a partner with the Priest, not only in the Cheat, but in the Advantages of it, and sometimes they officiate for one another. When this Artist is in the act of Conjuration, or of *Pauwawing*, as they term it, he always appears with an Air of Haste, or else in some convulsive posture, that seems to strain all the Faculties, like the Sybils, when they pretended to be under the power of Inspiration."—*History of Virginia*, p. 183.

Stanza V.

Loose o'er his frame the bear-skin hung.

"Of all the sights I ever saw among them, none appeared so near akin to what is usually imagined of *infernal powers*, as the appearance of one who was a devout and zealous reformer, or rather restorer, of what he supposed was the ancient religion of the Indians. He made his appearance in his pontifical garb, which was a coat of bear-skins, dressed with the hair on, and hanging down to his toes, a pair of bear-skin stockings, and a great wooden face," &c.—*Brainerd's Diary.* E.

"The Habit of the Indian Priest is a Cloak made in the Form of a Woman's Petticoat; but instead of tying it about their middle, they fasten the Gatherings about their neck, and tye it upon the Right Shoulder, always keeping one Arm out to use upon Occasion. This Cloak hangs even at the Bottom, but reaches no lower than the middle of the thigh; but what is most particular in it is, that it is constantly made of a Skin drest soft, with the Pelt or Fur on the Outside, and revers'd; insomuch, that when the Cloak has been a little worn, the Hair falls down in Flakes, and looks very shagged and Frightful."—*History of Virginia*, p. 143.

STANZA VI.

O saw ye that gleaming unearthly of light?

"Among their various superstitions, they [the Algonquins] believe that the vapour which is seen to hover over moist and swampy places, is the spirit of some person lately dead."—*M'Kenzie*. E.

STANZA VII.

Since earth from the deep—
Rose green o'er the waters.

See the first Note to Canto III. There are many varieties in the account of the creation, given by the Indians, all agreeing in the circumstance of the earth's emerging from the deep. It is unnecessary to quote them here.

He perished, the Mammoth.—

An Indian chief, of the Delaware tribe, who visited the Governor of Virginia, during the revolution, informed him "that it was a tradition handed down from their fathers, that in ancient times a herd of these tremendous animals came to the Bick-bone-licks, and began an universal destruction of the bear, deer, elk, buffalo, and other animals which had been created for the use of the Indians. That the great Man above, looking down and seeing this, was so enraged, that he seized his lightning, descended on the earth, seated himself on a neighbouring mountain, on a rock, (on which his seat and the prints of his feet are still to be seen,) and hurled his bolts among them, till the whole were slaughtered, except the big bull, who, presenting his forehead to the shafts, shook them off as they fell, but, missing one at length, it wounded him in the side, whereon, springing round, he bounded over the Ohio, the Wabash, the Illinois, and finally over the great lakes, where he is living at this day."—*Jefferson's Notes.*

Yohewah.

I have retained this word in the text, because it sounds well; and, for the purposes of poetry, it is of little consequence whether it be a significant word, or a mere series of guttural noises. Yo-he-woh, as it is written by Adair, is precisely the noise made by the sailors, when hauling together; and as the Indians used it during their most violent dances, it is likely that similar exertions produced similar sounds; the giving utterance to which, in some measure, alleviated the pain of the effort. No doubt an Indian, when chopping wood, makes the same sort of grunt that a white man does. In like manner, Allelujah, or the sound resembling it, which the Indians are said to utter, is no more to be derived from the Hebrew, than from the Greek ελελευ, or the Irish howl, Ullaloa, or the English Halloa.

Where now are the giants the soil who possest?

See the first chapter of Heckewelder's "Historical Account," &c. The tradition of the Lenapé is, that when their fathers crost the Mississippi, they met, on this side of it, with a nation called Alligewi, from whom, the author says, the Alleghany river and mountains received their name. "Many wonderful things are told of this famous people. They are said to have been remarkably stout and tall, and there is a tradition that there were giants among them; people of a much larger size than the tallest of the Lenapé. It is related that they had built to themselves regular fortifications, or entrenchments, from whence they would sally out, but were generally repulsed." Mr. H. describes two entrenchments he has seen. "Outside of the gateway of each of these two entrenchments, which lay within a mile of each other, were a number of large flat mounds, in which, the Indian pilot said, were buried hundreds of the slain Talligewi, whom I shall hereafter, with Col. Gibson, call Alligewi." The traces of gigantic feet, in different parts of the country, mentioned in several books, are ascribed to this people in the text.

Stanza VIII.

Lo! even now like some tree where a Spirit before, &c.

"Autrefois les Sauvages voisins de l'Acadie avoient dans leur Pays sur le bord de la Mer un Arbre extrémement vieux, dont ils racontoient bien des merveilles, et qu'on voyoit toujours chargé d'offrandes. La Mer ayant découvert toute sa racine, il se soûtint encore longtems presqu'en l'air contre la violence des vents et des flots, ce qui confirma ces Sauvages dans la pensée qu'il étoit le siége de quelque grand Esprit: sa chute ne fut pas même capable de les détromper, et tant qu'il en parut quelque bout de branches hors de l'eau, on lui rendit les mêmes honneurs, qu'avoit reçûs tout l'Arbre, lorsqu'il étoit sur pied."—*Charlevoix*, p. 349.

The simile of Lucan must occur to every classical reader:—

Qualis frugifero quercus sublimis in agro
Exuvias veteres populi, sacrata que gestans
Dona ducum; nec jam validis radicibus hærens,
Pondere fixa suo est; nudosque per aëra ramos
Effundens, trunco, non frondibus, efficit umbram.

Our nations, the children of earth.

See Mr. Heckewelder, chapter xxxiv. and Charlevoix, p. 344, and as before quoted, for the Indian ideas of the origin of mankind. The latter author mentions various and different accounts; one of which coincides with that of the former. According to both authors, the Indians only considered man as the first of animals. They had a future state for the souls of bears, &c. as well as for those of men. Mr. Heckewelder quotes this tradition from a MS. of the Reverend Christopher Pyrlæus: "That they [the Iroquois] had dwelt in the earth where it was dark, and where no sun did shine. That though they followed hunting, they ate mice, which they caught with their hands. That Gauawagahha, (one of them,) having accidentally found a hole to get out of the earth at, he went out, and that, in walking about on the earth, he found a deer, which he took back with him, and that, both on account of the meat tasting so very good, and the favourable description he had given them of the country above and on the earth, their mother, concluded it best for them all to come out; that accordingly they did so, and immediately set about planting corn, &c. That, however, the Nocharanorsul, that is, the *ground hog*, would not come out, but had remained in the ground as before." For this reason, they would not eat this animal. Mr. Heckewelder says that this tradition is common to the Iroquois and Lenapé. It resembles the account given by Aeschilus, of the state in which Prometheus found mankind :

῾Οι πρῶτα μὲν βλέποντες ἔβλεπον μάτην,
Κλύοντες οὐκ ἤκουον· ἀλλ᾽ ὀνειράτων
᾽Αλίγκιοι μορφαῖσι, τον μακρὸν χρόνον
῎Εφυρον εἰκῆ πάντα, κοὔτι πλινθυφεῖς
Δόμους προσείλους ἦσαν, οὐ ξυλουργίαν·
Κατώρυχες δ᾽ ἔναιον, ὥστ᾽ ἀήσυροι
Μύρμηκες, ἄντρων ἐν μυχοῖς ἀνηλίοις. κ. τ. λ.

Stanza X.

Like the swarms of the doves o'er the meads that descend.

"We imbarqued and made towards a meadow, in the neighbourhood of which, the Trees were covered with that sort of Fowl, more than with Leaves : For just then 'twas the season in which they retire from the North Countries, and repair to the Southern Climates ; and one would have thought that all the Turtle-Doves upon Earth had chose to pass through this place. For the eighteen or twenty days that we stay'd there, I firmly believe that a thousand men might have fed upon 'em heartily, without putting themselves to any trouble."—*La Hontan*, i. p. 62.

"L'antre Manne, dont j'ai parlé, est une espece de Ramiers, qui passent ici dans les mois de Mai et de Juin ; on dit qu'autrefois ils obscurcissoient l'Air par leur multitude ; mais ce n'est plus la même chose aujourd'hui. Il en vient encore néanmoins jusqu' aux environs des Villes un assez grand nombre se reposer sur les arbres. On les appelle communément *Tourtes*, et ils different en effet des Ramiers, des Tourterelles et des Pigeons d'Europe, assez pour en faire une quatriéme espece. Ils sont plus petits que nos plus gros Pigeons, dont ils ont les Yeux, et les Nuances de la Gorge. Leur Plumage est d'un brun obscur, a l'exception des Ailes, où il y a des plumes d'un très-bien Bleu. On diroit que ces Oiseaux ne cherchent qu'à se faire tuer ; car s'il y a quelque Branche séche à un Arbre, c'est celle-là, qu'ils choisissent pour se percher, et ils se rangent de maniere, que le plus mal-adroit Tireur en peut abattre une demie douzaine au moins d'un seul coup de Fusil."—*Charlevoix*, p. 171.

STANZA XI.

Like the plants which by pure hands of virgins alone
Must be plucked.

"L'on montre certaines Plantes fort salutaires, qui n'ont point de virtu, disent les Sauvages, si elles ne sont employées par des mains vierges."—*Id.* 350.

The foul bird of avarice.

The Hawk. See a Note to the first Canto.

STANZA XII.

The avenging Spirit's fiery breath
Had poured the withering storm of death, &c.

A superstition akin to this, is recorded in Carver's Travels, p. 30.

Stolen when polluted walls were razed, &c.

This being a sacrifice to evil spirits, its materials were supplied by the opposites to all that was esteemed holy. As it is founded in error and mistake, the following Notes are selected merely to show whence the ideas in the text were derived; and by no means to support them.

"The Indian women are remarkably decent during their periodical illness; those nations that are most remote from the European settlements, as the Nadowessies, &c. are more particularly attentive to this point; though they all without exception adhere in some degree to the same custom. In every camp or town there is an apartment appropriated for their retirement at this time, to which they retreat, and seclude themselves with the utmost strictness, during this period, from all society," &c.—*Carver.* The rest of the passage with respect to the polluted fires is extracted in the Notes to Canto First. The author in another place, says, that these houses were fired, and immediately abandoned. See also *M'Kenzie, Adair,* &c.

STANZA XIV.

The Powwahs, &c.

"The manner of their devotion was, to kindle large fires in their wigwams, or in the open fields, and to sing and dance round them in a wild and violent manner. Sometimes they would all shout aloud, with the most antic and hideous notes. They made rattles of shells, which they shook, in a wild and violent manner, to fill up the confused noise. Their priests, or powahs, led in these exercises. They were dressed in the most odd and surprising manner, with skins of odious and frightful creatures about their heads, faces, arms, and bodies. They painted themselves in the most ugly forms which could be devised. They sometimes sang, and then broke forth into strong invocations, with starts, and strange motions and passions. When these ceased, the other Indians groaned, making wild and doleful sounds. At these times they sacrificed their skins, Indian money, and the best of their treasures. These were taken by their Powahs, and all cast into the fires and consumed together. The English were also persuaded that they, sometimes, sacrificed their children, as well as their most valuable commodities. Milford people observing an Indian child, nearly at one of these times of their devotion, dressed in an extraordinary manner, with all kinds of Indian finery, had the curiosity to inquire what could be the reason. The Indians answered that it was to be sacrificed, and the people supposed that it was given to the devil. The Evil Spirit which the New-England Indians called Hobbam-ocko, [or Hobam-oqui] the Virginia Indians called Okee. So deluded were these unhappy people, that they believed these barbarous sacrifices to be absolutely necessary. They imagined that, unless they appeased and conciliated their gods in this manner, they would neither suffer them to have peace, nor harvests." *Trumbull*, I. p. 49. The Historian of Connecticut, on the authority of Mather, and Purchas, thus assents to the popular belief with regard to the custom of human sacrifices among the Indians. In page 51, he has this passage,—" The stoutest and most promising boys were chosen, and trained up with peculiar care, in the observation of certain Indian rites and customs. They were kept from all delicious meats, trained to coarse fare, and made to drink the juice of bitter herbs, until it occasioned violent vomitings. They were beaten over their legs and shins with sticks, and made to run through brambles and thickets, to make them hardy, and, as the Indians said, to render them more acceptable to Hobbamocko." This is undoubtedly the same custom mentioned in the previous extract; and is precisely that which prevailed among the Indians of

Virginia, as seen by Captain John Smith, and which he thought was a sacrifice to the devil. His account is preserved in Purchas, and in the History of Virginia; and is explained in the latter book, by the ceremony of Huskanawing. See a Note to Canto First. Heckewelder calls it the *Initiation of Boys;* and Charlevoix, "getting a tutelary Genius," iii. p. 346. See the notes to the Rev. Dr. Jarvis' Discourse; where most of the authorities on this subject are quoted. It is fully manifest, that there was no such thing as the sacrifice of children, among our Indians. The plot of the poem was hastily formed, when we had scarcely read any thing on the manners of the Indians, or even the history of the times. This ignorance led us, not only to introduce a rite, which never had any existence, but to ascribe to Philip a useless piece of treachery and cruelty, with scarcely any necessity for it, even in supporting the fiction. I have endeavoured to make the incantations consistent with themselves, and with the error we fell into. As originally written, by myself, they did not possess even that merit. It is unnecessary to quote more from the old writers on the New-England Indians, to show their belief on this subject. They all agree, pretty much in the same point. " 'Tis an usual thing for them," says Mather, "to have their Assemblies, wherein, after the usage of some Diabolical *Rites,* a *Devil* appears unto them, to inform them and advise them about their circumstances; and sometimes there are odd Events of their making these applications to the *Devil.* For instance, 'tis particularly affirmed, That the *Indians* in their wars with us, finding a sore inconvenience by our *Dogs,*—sacrificed a *Dog* to the Devil; after which no *English* Dog would bark at an *Indian* for divers months ensuing."—*Magnalia,* iii. 192. What interpreter the Devil had on these occasions, does not appear. That he did not understand the Indian tongue, is manifest from what our author says himself, immediately after. "Once finding that the *Dæmons* in a possessed young Woman, understood the *Latin* and *Greek* and *Hebrew* Languages, my Curiosity led me to make Trial of this *Indian* Language, and the *Dæmons* did seem as if they did not understand it." Daniel Gookin gives this account of the matter. "Their religion is as other gentiles are. Some for their God, adore the Sun; others the moon; some the earth; others the fire; and like vanities. [This is confounding the Spirits, or ministerial agencies, with the One Supreme Being, whom the Indians undoubtedly worshipped, as the writer goes on to say.] Yet generally they acknowledge One great supreme doer of good; and him they call Wonand, or Mannitt: another that is the great doer of evil or mischief; and him they call Mattand, which is the devil; and him they dread and fear, *more* than they love and honour the former chief good, which is God. There are among them certain men and women, whom they call powows. These are partly wizards and witches, holding familiarity with Satan, that evil one; and partly are physicians, and make use, at least in show, of herbs and roots, for curing the sick and diseased, &c. The powows are reputed, and I conceive justly, to hold familiarity with the devil; and therefore are, by the English laws, prohibited the exercise of their diabolical practices within the English jurisdiction, under the penalty of five pounds,—and the procurer, five pounds,—and every person present, twenty pence. Satan doth strongly endeavour to keep up this practice among the Indians, and these powows are lactors for the devil," &c.—*Gookin*, p. 14.

Even Charlevoix believed in this absurd superstition. "Il est encore vrai que les Jongleurs rencontrent trop souvent juste dans leurs Prédictions, pour croire qu'ils devinent toujours par hazard, et qu'il se passe dans ces occasions des choses, qu'il n'est presque pas possible d'attribuer à aucun secret naturel. On a vû les pieux dont ces Etuves étoient fermées, se courber jusqu'a terre tandis que le Jongleur se tenoit tranquille, sans remuer, sans y toncher, qu'il chantoit, et qu'il prédisoit l'avenir. Les Lettres des anciens Missionaires sont remplies de faits, qui ne laissent aucun doute que ces Seducteurs n'ayent un veritable commerce avec le Pere de la seduction et du mensonge."—III. 362.

Some writers, on the contrary, have gone too far, in asserting that the Indians had no knowledge of the Evil Spirit. The prophet, mentioned by Brainerd, who pretended to restore the ancient religion of the Indians, told him "that there was no such creature as the devil, known among the Indians of old times." Baron La Hontan very drily remarks, "that, in speaking of the devil, they do not mean that Evil Spirit that in Europe is represented under the figure of a Man, with a long Tail, and great Horns and Claws." His conclusion on the subject appears to be correct—"that these

Ecclesiasticks, [Jugglers,] did not understand the true import of that great word, *Matchi Manitou.* For by the Devil they understand such things as are offensive to 'em, which, in our language, comes near to the signification of Misfortune, Fate, Unfavourable Destiny, &c." It was to *deprecate* the wrath of these baleful agencies, and not to *conciliate* their friendship and court their alliance, that sacrifices were offered to them.—*History of Virginia,* 170. The Indian worship extended to all the objects of nature. The Spirits of groves, torrents, mountains, rivers and caves, had all their adorers and oblations. The minutest and most contemptible particle of matter, by the craft of the Juggler, or sickly fancy of the patient, became a genius, and was connected with a magic spell. How far their philosophy went, in the adoration of moral influences, seems more questionable; and, though they are said to be believers in destiny, their worship of Fate, which La Hontan seems to imply, is highly improbable. As to their *Witchcraft,* no doubt its professors may have pretended a familiarity with the powers of evil. Their tricks were as simple and ridiculous, and often as fatal, as those of the practisers of the Obeah art, among the negroes.

Save their girdles rude from the otter torn, &c.

"The Conjuror shaves all his Hair off, except the crest on the crown; upon his Ear he wears the Skin of some dark-colored Bird; he, as well as the Priest, is commonly grim'd with Soot, or the like; he hangs an Otter skin at his girdle," &c. "He has a black Bird, with expanded wings, fastened to his Ear."—*History of Virginia,* 143, 183. "Les os et les Peaux des Serpens servent aussi beaucoup aux Jongleurs et aux Sorciers, pour faire leurs prestiges; et ils se font des bandeaux et des Ceintures de leurs Peaux." "Un Jongleur paroit ensuite, ayant à la main un bâton orné de plumes, par le moyen duquel il se vantoit de deviner les choses les plus cachées." —*Charlevoix.* The chichicoe, or chichicou, is a rattle, made of different materials, sometimes of a gourd, &c. It generally formed the music of a *powowing* assembly, and is mentioned under the same name by many different writers. See *Carver, Charlevoix, History of Virginia,* &c. "He advanced toward me with the instrument in his hand, that he used for music in his idolatrous worship, which was a dry *tortoise shell,* with some corn in it, and the neck of it drawn on a piece of wood, which made a very convenient handle."—*Brainerd's Diary.* E. The mode of painting the bodies, described in the text, is mentioned by *Carver* and *Charlevoix.*

STANZA XV.

A woman once.

The Indian women are described as peculiarly addicted to the worship of evil spirits.—*Charlevoix*, pp. 359, 360.

STANZA XVI.

And now began the Initiates' Dance.

The term "Initiate" is borrowed from Carver. He uses it, however, in reference to those who were admitted into "The Friendly Society of the Spirit."—p. 175. He mentions, in the same place, the Pawwah, or Black Dance, by which the Devil was supposed to be raised. The Dances of the Indians are described in so many places, and their mode is so well known, that I shall only insert the note left by my friend, from the *Diary of Brainerd.*

"Lord's day, Sept. 21.—I spent the day with the Indians on the island. As soon as they were up in the morning, I attempted to instruct them, and laboured to get them together, but quickly found they had something else to do; for they gathered together all their powwows, and set about half a dozen of them to playing their tricks, and acting their frantic postures, in order to find out why they were so sickly, numbers of them being at that time disordered with a fever and bloody flux. In this they were engaged for several hours, making all the wild, distracted motions imaginable; sometimes singing, sometimes howling, sometimes extending their hands to the utmost stretch, spreading all their fingers, and seemed to push with them, as if they designed to fright something away, or at least keep it at arm's end; sometimes sitting flat on the earth; then bowing down their faces to the ground; wringing their sides, as if in pain and anguish; twisting their faces, turning up their eyes, grunting or puffing. These monstrous actions seemed to have something in them peculiarly suited to raise the devil, if he could be raised by any thing odd and frightful. Some of them were much more fervent in the business than others, and seemed to chant, peep, and mutter, with a great degree of warmth and vigor. I sat about thirty feet from them, (though undiscovered,) with my Bible in my hand, resolving, if possible, to spoil their sport, and prevent their receiving any answer from the infernal world." E.

Then pealed the loud hah-hah!

" Hoh, hoh, hoh,—These notes, if they might be so termed, are articulated with a harsh accent, and strained out with the utmost force of their lungs." "Whoo, Whoo, Whoop, is continued in a long, shrill tone, nearly till the breath is exhausted, and then broken off with a sudden elevation of the voice."—*Carver*, 172, 217.

STANZA XVII.

Beyond the hills the Spirit sleeps.

The Sun was often worshipped as the visible God. In the most solemn sacrifices, the fire was sometimes kindled from his heat. —*Carver, La Hontan, Vol. Second.* The Hurons are said to have confounded Areskoui with the Sun.—*Charlevoix.* When the Sun has set, they say he is dead.—*Carver, Charlevoix,* iii. 219. *Adair,* 76.

The Wakon Cave.

See a Note in Canto First, and on the "Wakon-Bird," in the Notes to Canto Second.

STANZA XVIII.

Your serpent scar
On the blasted trunk is graven.

" Ces Peuples ne connoissent pas mieux la nature du Tonnerre; quelques uns le prenoient pour la voix d'une espéce particuliere d'Hommes, qui voloient dans les airs: d'autres disoient que ce bruit venoit de certains Oiseaux, qui leur étoient inconnus. Selon les Montaguais, c'etoit l'effort, que faisoit une Génie pour vomir une Couleuvre, qu'il avoit avalée; et ils appuyoient ce sentiment sur ce que, quand le Tonnerre étoit tombé sur un Arbre, on y voyoit une figure assez approchante de celle d'une Couleuvre." —*Charlevoix*, iii. 401.

The other superstitions referred to in this Stanza, being local, and some of them belonging, moreover, to the Hurons, are far-fetched for an Incantation of the New-England Powaws.—*Transeant cum cæteris.* " Nearly half way between Saganaum Bay and the north-west corner of the Lake, lies another, which is termed Thunder Bay. The Indians, who have frequented these parts from time immemorial, and every European traveller that has passed through it, have unanimously agreed to call it by this name."—*Carver*, 91. "One of the Chipeway chiefs told me that some of their people, being once driven on the island of Maurepas, found on it large quantities of heavy, shining, yellòw sand, that, from their description, must have been gold dust. Being struck with the beautiful appearance of it, in the morning, when they re-entered their canoe, they attempted to bring some away; but a spirit, of an amazing size, according to their account, sixty feet in height, strode in the water after them, and commanded them to deliver back what they had taken away. Since this incident, no Indian that has ever heard of it, will venture near the same haunted coast."—*Idem*, 85. This Island is known by the name of Manataulin, which signifies a Place of Spirits, and is considered by the Indians as sacred as those already mentioned in Lake Superior. Two small islands near Detroit were called 'les Isles de Serpens à Sonnettes;' Charlevoix says, "on assûre qu'elles sont tellement remplies de ces Animaux, que l'Air en est infecté." Serpent worship was common to all the Indians, but more peculiarly cultivated among some nations, as the Malhomines.—*Charlevoix*, 291.

STANZA XIX.

Come ye hither who o'er the thatch
Of the coward murderer hold your watch.

"Les Hurons étendoient le corps mort sur des Perches, au haut d'une Cabanne, et le Meurtrier étoit obligé de se tenir plusieurs jours de suite immédiatement au dessous, et de recevoir tout ce qui découloit de ce Cadavre, non-seulement sur soi, mais encore sur son manger, qu'on mettoit auprès de lui, à moins que par un présent considérable, fait à la Cabanne du Défunt il n'obtînt de garantir ses Vivres de ce Poison."—*Charlevoix*, iii. p. 274.

STANZA XX.

Come ye who give power
To the curse that is said, &c.

"On a vû des Filles s'étrangler, pour avoir reçû une réprimande assez légere de leurs Meres, ou quelques gouttes d'Eau au Visage, et l'en avertir en lui disant, *Tu n'auras plus de Fille.*" —*Id.* 226.

STANZA XXI.

Come ye who as hawks hover o'er
The spot where the war club is lying.

As a commencement of hostilities, according to Heckewelder, the Indians murder one of the enemy, and leave the war club lying near the body; it is painted with their devices, that the party attacked may know their enemies, and not execute revenge on an innocent tribe.—*Page* 165.

STANZA XXII.

Ye who at the sick man's bed, &c.

As before mentioned, sickness is always ascribed to the agency of some spirit, of whatever form the Juggler's fancy pleases, which must be driven out of the patient, before his recovery can be effected. If the force of imagination, in sickness, be duly considered, the practice of treating all diseases as cases of hypochondria, may not be so ridiculous, as the fantastic manœuvres of these quacks would, at first sight, imply.

STANZA XXIII.

And ye who delight,
The soul to affright, &c.

"Ils disent que l'Ame séparée du corps conserve les mêmes inclinations, qu'elle avoit auparavant, et c'est la raison pourquoi ils enterrent avec les Morts tout ce qui étoit a leur usage." "Les Ames lorsque le tems est venu qu'elles doivent se séparer pour toujours de leurs corps, vont dans une Région, qui est destinée pour être leur demeure éternelle. Cette Région, disent les Sauvages, est fort éloignée vers l'Occident, et les Ames mettent plusieurs mois à s'y rendre. Elles ont même de grandes difficultés a surmonter, et elles courent de grands risques, avant que d'y arriver." "Dans le Pays des Ames, selon quelques-uns, l'Ame est transformée en Tourterelle."—*Charlevoix*, pp. 351, 352.

STANZA XXV.

Not beneath the mantle blue,
Spread below Yohewah's feet, &c.

Sacrifices to good Spirits were made, when the sky was clear, the air serene, &c.—*La Hontan*, ii. 31, 32.

O serpent God.

This is one of the forms under which the Indians supposed the Evil Spirit to appear. "Another power they worship whom they call Hobbamock, and to the northward of us Hobbamoqui; this as farre as wee can conceive is the devill; him they call upon to cure their wounds and diseases. This Hobbomock appears in sundry formes unto them, as in the shape of a man, a deare, a fawne, an eagle, &c., but most ordinarily as a Snake."—*Winslow's 'Good News from New-England,' Anno* 1622, *in Purchas*, iv. p. 1867. And see *ante*, Notes on this Canto.

STANZA XXVIII.

The hawks high are roving.

"Before a thunder-shower these birds [night-hawks] are seen at an amazing height in the air, assembled together in great numbers."—*Carver.*

The Elk-skin about him,
The Crow-skin above.

It has been already mentioned, that the skin of some dark coloured bird was made use of at all conjurations. The Elk-skin was also employed, according to Carver and others. Charlevoix says that it was always considered a good omen, to dream of the Elk.

NOTES TO CANTO FIFTH.

STANZA II.

Where yon old elm its arm extends, &c.

"They also fancy another spirit which appears in the shape of a man, upon the trees near the lodge of a person deceased, whose property has not been interred with them. He is represented as bearing a gun in his hand, and it is believed that he does not return to his rest, until the property that has been withheld from the grave has been sacrificed to it."—*M'Kenzie's Hist. of the Fur Trade*, p. 74.

STANZA VI.

Like some lone bird whose pinions hover, &c.

M. de Champlain remarked, among the fishes in the Lake which bears his name, one called by the savages *Chaousarou*, which is termed by Charlevoix "Le Poisson Armé." "Il a le corps à peu près de la figure d'un Brochet; mais il est couvert d'une Ecaille à l'épreuve du Poignard: sa couleur est d'un gris argenté, et il lui sorte de dessous la Gueule une Arête platte, dentelée, creuse et percée par le bout, &c. Un tel Animal est un vrai Pirate parmi les Habitans des Eaux; mais on n'imagineroit peutêtre pas qu'il fait aussi la Guerre aux Habitans des Airs; il la fait néanmoins, et en habile Chasseur; voici comment. Il se cache dans les Roseaux, de telle sorte qu'on ne peut voir que son Arme, qu'il tient élevée perpendiculairement au-dessus de l'Eau. Les Oiseaux, qui viennent pour se reposer, prennent cette Arme pour un Roseau sec, ou un morceau de Bois, et se perchent dessus. Ils n'y sont pas plûtôt, que la Poisson ouvre la Gueule, et fait si subitement le mouvement nécessaire pour ravir sa Proye, que rarement elle lui échape, &c."—*Charlevoix*, p. 153.

Even the vile fox's part essay.

The fox is said by Charlevoix, to play the part of jackall, for the Carcajou, or Quincajou, as it is termed by him.

STANZA IX.

The Carcajou about him dart.

"This creature, which is of the cat kind, is a terrible enemy to the deer, elk, moose, carraboo, &c. He either comes upon them from some concealment unperceived, or climbs up into a tree, and waits till one of them, driven by an extreme of heat or cold, takes shelter under it; when he fastens upon his neck, and opening the jugular vein, soon brings his prey to the ground. This he is enabled to do by his long tail, with which he encircles the body of his adversary; and the only means they have to shun their fate, is by flying immediately to the water; by this method, as the Carcajou has a great dislike to that element, he is sometimes got rid of before he can effect his purpose."—*Carver.*

STANZA XII.

Low in the swamp's unequal ground, &c.

This is an error, which I omitted to correct. The Indians were not in the swamp, but on an upland, as is mentioned, correctly, in the Sixth Canto.

STANZA XIV.

Tradition meet for vulgar faith, &c.

Philip was said to have seen the devil, in a dream, the night before he was killed. Hubbard merely notices it in a parenthesis. "Whether the devil appeared to him in a dream that night as he did unto Saul, foreboding his tragical end, it matters not." Increase Mather says,—"It seemeth that night *Philip* (like the man in the Host of *Midian*) dreamed that he was fallen into the hands of the English, and just as he was saying to those that were with him, that they must fly for their lives that day, lest the Indian that was gone from him should discover where he was, Our Souldiers came upon him," &c. Cotton Mather borrows the account from his namesake. "That very night *Philip* (like the Man in the Army of Midian) had been dreaming that he was *fall'n into the hands of the English*," &c. Connecting the story of the dream, with what Mather says Philip's Powaws had told him,—with the vision said to be revealed during the ceremony of Huskanawing,—and t e belief in Destiny, which the Indians are said by Adair to entertain,—I have endeavoured to make some poetical use of those several superstitions; and to give some unity to that part of the plot, which is taken from history. I have made Ahauton shoot Philip; though that exploit is said, by Increase Mather, to have been performed by a Pocasset Indian, named *Alderman* by the English.

There was a tradition, that Philip and the Devil used to amuse themselves, during their nocturnal interviews, by pitching quoits, from the top of Mount Hope to Popasquash neck. I have understood, that some large flat stones are still to be seen, at the latter place, which are singularly situated; and that the mark of a large foot is visible somewhere on the rocks, in the vicinity of Mount Ho e, which was once attributed to the impress of the Devil.

Stanza XV.

Massasoiet—Ouamsutta—Uncompoën.

See the Notes to Canto First.

Calumets.

Carver says he knows not why the Pipe of Peace was so termed by the French. La Hontan, in his explanatory Table, says,—"Calumet in general signifies a Pipe, being a *Norman* Word, deriv'd from Chalumeau. The Savages do not understand this Word. The Pipe of Peace is called in the Iroquese Language *Ganondaoë*, and by the other Savage Nations *Poagem*."

Flutes and tabours.

The Indians had rude musical instruments, resembling these. To the south, as might be expected, their music was more tolerable, or rather, less execrable, than in the north. See *Bartram's Travels.*

Stanza XVI.

Assawomsett's lake—Sausaman.

See Notes to Canto First.

STANZA XVII.

Metapoiset's forest—Weetamoe.

"August 6. Twenty Souldiers marched out of Taunton, and took all those Indians, in number thirty and six, only the *Squaw-Sachem of Pocasset*, who was next unto *Philip*, in respect of the mischief that hath been done, and the blood that hath been shed in this Warr, escaped alone; but not long after some of *Taunton* finding an Indian Squaw in *Metapoiset* newly dead, cut off her head, aud it hapned to be *Weetamoo*, i. e. *Squaw Sachem* her *head*. When it was set upon a pole in *Taunton*, the Indians who were prisoners there, knew it presently, and made a most horrid and diabolical Lamentation, crying out that it was their Queen's head. Now here it is to be observed, that God himself, by his own hand, brought this enemy to destruction. For in that place, where, the last year, she furnished *Philip* with Canooes for his men, she herself could not meet with a Canoo, but venturing over the River upon a Raft, that brake under her, so that she was drowned, just before the English found her. Surely *Philip's* turn will be next." —*Increase Mather*, pp. 45, 46.

STANZA XXII.

The belief in a metempsychosis, which Philip is here made to express, is not unwarranted.—" I once took great pains to dissuade from these notions a very sensible Indian. He asserted very strange things of his own supernatural knowledge, which he had obtained not only at the time of his initiation, but at other times, even before he was born. He said he knew he had lived through two generations; that he had died twice and was born a third time, to live out the then present race, after which he was to die, and never more to come to this country again. He well remembered what the women had predicted, while he was yet in his mother's womb," &c. &c.—*Heckewelder*, p. 240.

"The Indians call this Altar by the Name of Powcorance, from whence proceeds the great Reverence they have for a small Bird that uses the Woods, and in their Note continually sound that Name. They say this is the Soul of one of their Princes; and on that score, they would not hurt it for the World."—*History of Virginia*, p. 185.—" The Chepewyans have some faint notion of the transmigration of the soul, so that if a child be born with teeth, they instantly imagine, from its premature appearance, that it bears a resemblance to some person who had lived to an advanced period, and that he has assumed a renovated life, with these extraordinary tokens of maturity."—*M'Kenzie. History of the Fur Trade*, 24.

" They brought me word that some new married Women were running to receive the Soul of an old Fellow that lay a dying. From thence I concluded, that the People were *Pythagoreans;* and upon that Apprehension, ask'd 'em how they came to eat Animals, into which their Souls might be transfus'd: But they made answer, that the Transmigration of Souls is always confin'd to the respective Species, so that the Soul of a Man cannot enter into a Fowl, or that of a Fowl cannot be lodged in a quadruped, and so on." *La Hontan*, I. 120.

" D'autres reconnoissent dans tous les Hommes deux Ames; ils attribuent à l'une tout ce que je viens de dire, ils prétendent que l'autre ne quitte jamais le corps, si ce n'est pour passer dans un autre; ce qui n'arrive pourtant guéres, disent-ils, qu'aux Ames des Enfans, lesquelles ayant peu joui de la vie, obtiennent d'en recommencer une nouvelle," &c.—*Charlevoix*, p. 351.

STANZA XXIII.

No wingëd sorcerer, &c.

" The Fish Hawk skims over the lakes and rivers, and sometimes seems to lie expanded on the water, as he hovers so close to it, and having, by some attractive power, drawn the fish within its reach, darts suddenly upon them. The charm it makes use of is supposed to be an oil contained in a small bag in the body," &c. —*Carver.*

No charmed bough, &c.

The Witch Hazel has been supposed to have the property of detecting veins of precious metal. The superstition is improperly introduced in the speech of an Indian.—T. C. C.

To see the foul and senseless beast,
On generous valour coldly feast.

" However remarkable it may appear, it is certain, that though the venom of the rattle-snake affects, in a greater or less degree, all animated nature, the *hog* is an exception to the rule, as that animal will readily destroy them, without dreading their poisonous fangs, and fatten on their flesh."—*Carver.*

STANZA XXVI. Ver. 3.

Along the mist-clad mountain's brow, &c.

Carver, (page 265,) gives a beautifully characteristic account of the conduct of an Indian woman, on the successive deaths of her son and husband. The third verse, in the death-song of Philip, is taken from her Lament. "If thou hadst continued with us, my dear Son, how well would the bow have become thy hand, and how fatal would thine arrows have proved to the enemies of our band. Thou wouldst often have drank their blood, and eaten their flesh,* and numerous slaves would have rewarded thy toils. With a nervous arm wouldst thou have seized the wounded buffaloe, or have combatted the fury of the enraged bear. Thou wouldst have overtaken the flying elk, and have kept pace on the mountain's brow with the fleetest deer," &c.

Ver. 4. *Say, have I left ye, champions brave!*

"The bones of our deceased countrymen lie uncovered; they call out to us to revenge their wrongs, and we must satisfy their request. Their spirits cry out against us. They must be appeased. Sit, therefore, no longer inactive; give way to the impulse of your natural valour, anoint your hair, paint your faces, fill your quivers; let the forests resound with your songs; console the spirits of the dead, and tell them they shall be revenged."—*Carver,* p. 195.

STANZA XXVII.

Tiask. Tespiquin. Annawan.

Tiask, or Tiash, Tespiquin, Totoson, and others, were Philip's chief counsellors. Those mentioned in the text were with him in the swamp. They were all caught and killed soon after. Annawan,

---

* These Indian metaphors, it is well known, are not to be taken literally. They mean no more than killing their enemies, simply; though several stories are related of the literal execution of their threats, "that they would suck the blood of their enemies." *Uncas* is said to have eaten a piece of Miantonimo. But the authority is very questionable.

or Annawon, was also a chief captain and counsellor, and seems to have been an intelligent and high-minded warrior. He was taken by Captain Church, soon after his escape from the swamp, where Philip was killed; and behaved with great composure and magnanimity, after his capture. "He was put to death, as he justly had deserved," says Mr. Hubbard.

NOTES TO CANTO SIXTH.

Thee, Indians tell, the first of men to win,
Clomb long the vaulted heaven's unmeasured height.

The Iroquois do not go back to the earth, for the creation of man. Six men first appear in their mythology; one of whom ascended to heaven to seek a woman, named Atahansic. He found her; and when she was detected in having received his visit, she was precipitated from the upper regions. She alighted on the back of a Tortoise, where she was delivered of twins, one of whom killed the other, &c.—*Charlevoix*, p. 344.

Thou weeping comest, the sweet sagamité to strow.

" Chacun se retire ensuite chez soi, mais des Femmes reviennent pendant quelques jours verser au même endroit de la Sagamité." —*Idem*, p. 378. Sagamité is a mixture of Indian corn and other ingredients.

Stanza XVI.

The account of the ambushment and death of Philip, is taken from Captain Church.

"By that time they were got over the ferry, and came near the ground, half the night was spent. The Captain commands a halt, and bringing the company together, he asked Major *Sandford's* and Captain *Golding's* advice, what method was best to take in making the onset, but they declined giving him any advice, telling him, *That his great experience and success forbid their taking upon them to give advice.* Then Captain *Church* offered Captain *Golding* that he should have the honour (if he would please to accept of it) to beat up *Philip's* head quarters. He accepted the offer, and had his allotted number drawn out to him, and the pilot. Captain *Church's* instructions to him were to be very careful in his approach to the enemy, and be sure not to shew himself until by day light they might see and discern their own men from the enemy ; told him also, that his custom in the like cases was, to creep, with his company, on their bellies, until they came as near as they could ; and that as soon as the enemy discovered them they would cry out ; and that was the word for his men to fire and fall on. Directed him, when the enemy should start, and take into the swamp, they should pursue with speed, every man shouting and making what noise they could ; for he would give orders to his ambuscade to fire on any that should come silently.

" Captain *Church* knowing that it was *Philip's* custom to be foremost in the flight, went down to the swamp, and gave Capt. *Williams* of *Scituate* the command of the right wing of the ambush, and placed an *Englishman* and an Indian together behind such shelters of trees, &c. that he could find, and took care to place them at such distance that none might pass undiscovered between them ; charged them to be careful of themselves, and of hurting their friends, and to fire at any that should come silently thro' the swamp ; but being somewhat further thro' the swamp than he was aware of, he wanted men to make up his ambuscade. Having placed what men he had, he took Major *Sandford* by the hand, said *Sir, I have so placed them that it is scarce possible* Philip *should escape them.* The same moment a shot whistled over their heads, and then the noise of a gun towards *Philip's* camp. Captain *Church* thought at first it might be some gun fired by accident ; but before he could speak, a whole volley followed, which was earlier than he expected. One of *Philip's* gang going forth, looked round him, and Captain *Golding* tho't the Indian looked right at him, (though probably it was but his conceit) so fired at him, and upon his firing, the whole company that were with him fired upon the enemies' shelter, before the Indians had time to rise from their sleep, and so overshot them. But their shelter was open on that side next the swamp, built so on purpose for the convenience of flight on occasion. They were soon in the swamp, and *Philip* the foremost, who starting at the first gun, threw his petunk and powder-horn over his head, catch'd up his gun, and ran as fast as he could scamper, without any more clothes than his small breeches and stockings, and ran directly on two of Capt. *Church's* ambush; they let him come fair within shot, and the Englishman's gun missing fire, he bid the Indian fire away, and he did so to purpose, sent one musket bullet through his heart, and another not above two inches from it; he fell upon his face in the mud and water, with his gun under him. By this time the enemy perceived they were waylaid on the east side of the swamp, tack'd about short. One of the enemy, who seemed to be a great surly old fellow, halloo'd with a loud voice, and often called out, *Iootash, Iootash.* Captain *Church* called to his Indian *Peter,* and asked him, *who that was that call'd so?* He answered, It was old *Annawon, Philip's* great Captain, calling on his soldiers to stand to it, and fight stoutly. Now the enemy finding that place of the swamp which was not ambush'd, many of them made their escape in the *English* tracks. The man that had shot down *Philip,* ran with all speed to Capt. *Church,* and inform'd him of his exploit, who commanded him to be silent about it, and let no man more know it, until they had drove the swamp clean; but when they had drove the swamp thro', and found the enemy had escaped, or at least the most of them, and the sun now up, and so the dew gone, that they could not easily track them, the whole company met together at the place where the enemies' night shelter was; and then Captain *Church* gave them the news of *Philip's* death; upon which the whole army gave three loud huzzas. Captain *Church* ordered his body to be pulled out of the mire on to the upland, so some of Captain *Church's* Indians took hold of him by his stockings, and some by his small breeches, (being otherwise naked) and drew him thro' the mud to the upland, and a doleful, great, naked, dirty beast he looked like. Captain *Church* then said, *That forasmuch as he had caused many an* Englishman's *body to be unburied, and to rot above ground, that not one of his bones should be buried.* And calling his old Indian executioner, bid him behead and quarter him; accordingly he came with his hatchet and stood over him, but before he struck he made a small speech, directing it to *Philip;* and then went to work, and did as he was ordered. *Philip* having one very remarkable hand, being much scarred, occasioned by the splitting of a pistol in it formerly; Captain *Church* gave the head and that hand to *Alderman,* the Indian who shot him, to shew such Gentlemen as would bestow gratuities upon him; and accordingly he got many a penny by it. This was in the latter end of August, 1676."—*Church's History*, pp. 70, 71, 72, 73.

The death of Philip draws from Captain Church no other comment, than that his company got but four shillings and sixpence a piece for their trouble. They shot but few Indians, and Philip's head went with the rest, at thirty shillings each.

There is a comical history, of the Discovery of America, and the Wars with the Indians, written by one H. Trumbull, which seems to have gone through several editions. He states that Philip was lying in a swamp, near Mount Hope, with ninety *Seaconet* Indians, and was shot, by a *Mohegan*, on the *twenty-seventh of October*, 1679. Also, that Oneco, son of Uncas, broiled and ate a pound of Philip's flesh. Now the *Seaconets* were with Captain Church; Philip was shot by a *Pocasset* Indian; and that event took place on the *twelfth of August*, 1676. All the authorities agree in this point; and the story of Oneco and the pound of flesh, is an embellishment drawn entirely from the sanguinary imagination of this blundering chronicler. The rest of his history, at least as far as I am acquainted with the facts it professes to record, is equally, and as surprisingly, inaccurate.

STANZA XVII.

But as the elks in northern wood, &c.

The mode of hunting the elk, by driving him into the water, where other hunters are disposed in a semicircle of canoes, is described by *Charlevoix*, pp. 7. 126.

STANZA XXIV.

As amber gum to feverish vein.

The balm of the Sweet Gum Tree, or Liquid Amber, is reckoned by the Indians to be an excellent febrifuge.—*Carver*, 335.

It will be seen from the extract from Church, in what respect we have deviated from history. It is unnecessary to add any thing more to these notes; except that Philip's quarters were hung up, "and his head (in the words of Mather) carried in Triumph to Plymouth, where it arrived on the very day that the Church there was keeping a solemn Thanksgiving to God. God sent 'em in the Head of a Leviathan for a Thanksgiving Feast.

οὕτως πᾶς ἀπόλοιτο, ὅτις τοιαῦτάγε ῥέζοι.

Sic pereat quisquis captârit talia posthac!"

ERRATA.

Page 4, *l.* 13, *for* souless, *read* soulless.
153, *l.* 15, *for* murmurs, *read* summons.
183, *l.* 2, *for* krew, *read* knew.
188, *l.* 3, *for* where, *read* when.
Id. *l.* 4, *for* came *read* come.
189, *l.* 17, *for* Thy, *read* My, &c.

www.ingramcontent.com/pod-product-compliance
Lightning Source LLC
LaVergne TN
LVHW010201110826
845151LV00002B/572
* 9 7 8 1 4 2 5 5 3 6 1 4 5 *